SEASONED WITH RHYMES AND A PINCH OF THYME

IMMANUEL EVANGELICAL LUTHERAN CHURCH

BY
BONNIE R. HULL

To Julia,

Enjoy!

Bonnie

A MAPLE CREEK MEDIA BOOK

Printed in the United States of America

ISBN-13: 978-1-937004-01-9

ISBN-10: 1-937004-01-5

Maple Creek Media, a division of Old Line Publishing, LLC
P.O. Box 624
Hampstead, MD 21074
Toll-Free Phone: 1-877-866-8820
Toll-Free Fax: 1-877-778-3756
Email: oldlinepublishing@comcast.net
Website: www.oldlinepublishingllc.com

DEDICATION

This book is dedicated first to my Heavenly Father who gave me the talent and the time to devote myself to this venture. Secondly, I dedicate this book, on the 250th year celebration of our church, to the wonderful mothers and servants of Immanuel Evangelical Lutheran Church who have helped mold and nourish their families and friends, both physically and spiritually, by contributing to Immanuel. And, lastly, I dedicate this book to Pastor Ellis Kretschmer who encouraged me to write, as well as to compile the poems that have become a part of this book.

FOREWORD

Immanuel Evangelical Lutheran Church was started 250 years ago, log by log and later brick by brick. I was carried into this church as a babe in arms by my mother not remembering much of its early years, but fortunate to have been a part of its later growth from the 1950's.

As I look back on those years, I am so appreciative and grateful for having had the opportunity to be a part, as well as having learned to know some of the members and their families so personally through the composition of these poems.

I hope you will enjoy reading these as much as I have enjoyed writing them. In retyping the poems for this book, I have laughed and I have cried not realizing how much I truly miss many of these beautiful people who were pillars of our church and who were part of my "good ole days" at Immanuel.

As most of you are aware, Immanuel Lutheran Church is celebrating 250 years as a congregation. A lot of research has been done through the years to preserve our history, but there's one source, if it could talk, that could tell us everything about our heritage, and even more, and that is our old oak tree. The tree is over seven feet in circumference, its branches cover over ⅛ of an acre of ground, and it is over 325 years old.

Immanuel Lutheran Church has been referred to as "the mother congregation of Lutheranism in Carroll County" and when our charter was granted to begin our church, our oak tree was used as a landmark.

The proceeds from the sale of this book will be donated toward the continued preservation of the oak tree and in memory of Earl Yingling, who was a very respected tree man in Maryland, one of our church members, and who took care of our oak tree for many years.

TREES By Joyce Kilmer (1886-1918)

"I think that I shall never see,
A poem as lovely as a tree.
A tree whose hungry mouth is prest,
Against the earth's sweet flowing breast.
A tree that looks at God all day,
And lifts her leafy arms to pray.

A tree that may in summer wear,
A nest of robins in her hair.
Upon whose bosom snow has lain,
Who intimately lives with rain.
Poems are made by fools like me,
But only God can make a tree."

IMMANUEL EVANGELICAL LUTHERAN CHURCH

TABLE OF CONTENTS

TABLE OF CONTENTS

CHAPTER I

MOTHERS OF THE YEAR

1969 - 1989

INTRODUCTION

In 1969, Pastor Ellis Kretschmer came to Immanuel Evangelical Lutheran Church and began the tradition of acknowledging a special Mother of the Year at Immanuel each Mother's Day. In 1970, Pastor Kretschmer requested that I compose a poem depicting the life of our Mother of the Year to be used in her presentation on Mother's Day. Following, you will find these poems, along with some of her recipes, since our mothers were such wonderful cooks and also since I love cooking and collecting recipes.

Our Mother of the Year was selected by a committee of church officers and leaders. I was never a part of this committee, but I was told this was a very, very difficult decision. All of our Mothers of Immanuel are and have been so special to their families and Immanuel in the example they portrayed as wives, mothers, homemakers and as members of Immanuel in their nourishing of Christian love.

IMMANUEL EVANGELICAL LUTHERAN CHURCH

MAY 1969, IMMANUEL'S MOTHER OF THE YEAR
LILLIE ZUMBRUN

Mrs. Lillie Zumbrun was chosen as our first Mother of the Year, but I had not been requested to write the poems until 1970. She and her family were pillars of Immanuel and I wanted to acknowledge a truly wonderful mother.

Following is a recipe, which some of you may remember. It was a taffy-like candy that her nephew, Henry Hoffman, always looked forward to when visiting his aunt. Her niece, Gloria Armacost also remembers her delicious doughnuts that were a favorite with her family and friends.

Mrs. Zumbrun will also be remembered by me patting oysters for our oyster and turkey suppers. One year as a teenager and waiting on tables at our supper, her husband, Mr. Morris Zumbrun, inquired of me, when sitting down to eat, why I was not eating the fried oysters. I told him I couldn't stand to look at them. He said, "All you have to do is cover them with lots of ketchup and you'll never know they are there." Still, that's the only way I can eat a fried oyster.

We were very honored in 1984 that Mr. and Mrs. Zumbrun's son, Dr. Morris Zumbrun, was elected Bishop of the Maryland Synod. In 1984, Reverend and Mrs. Zumbrun transferred their membership back into Immanuel's congregation. In 1995, Bishop Zumbrun celebrated his 50th year of ordination. What a feeling this special mother must have had to see her son reach such a position in his life and it all began with her loving and nurturing him in a Christian home.

FROM THE KITCHEN OF: In Memory of Lillie Zumbrun by Lenora Hoffman
RECIPE FOR: Aunt Lillie's Candy
INGREDIENTS: 2 cups sugar
                 1 cup syrup
                 Butter size of walnut
                 2 tbsp. Vinegar

Cook until it spins a thread. Add nuts if desired and pour into buttered pan until cool.

FROM THE KITCHEN OF: Evelyn Zumbrun (wife of Bishop Morris Zumbrun, son of Lillie and Morris Zumbrun)
RECIPE FOR: Black Bottom Cupcakes
INGREDIENTS: 1½ cups flour 1 tsp. vanilla
                 ¼ cup cocoa 1 cup (8 oz.) cream cheese
                 ½ tsp. salt 1 egg
                 1 cup sugar ⅓ cup sugar
                 1 tsp. soda ⅛ tsp. salt
                 1 cup water 1 cup semi-sweet choc.
                 1 tbsp. vinegar morsels
                 ⅓ cup oil

Sift together dry ingredients in mixing bowl. Add water, vinegar, oil and vanilla. Fill cupcake liners ⅓ full. In a separate mixing bowl, mix cream cheese, egg, sugar, salt and chocolate chips. Top chocolate batter with a heaping teaspoon of cream cheese mixture. Bake at 350 degrees for 30 to 35 minutes. Sprinkle with sugar and chopped almonds, if desired.

FROM THE KITCHEN OF: Gloria Armacost (niece of Lillie and Morris Zumbrun)
RECIPE FOR: Cheese Soufflé
INGREDIENTS: 8 slices white bread

10 oz. stick mild Kraft Cheddar cheese
7 eggs
½ stick margarine, melted
2 cups milk
½ tsp. salt
Dash of pepper

Trim crust from bread and cube. Alternate layers of bread and cheese in an ungreased baking dish. Beat eggs well with mixer. Slowly add melted margarine and milk to eggs. Add salt and pepper. Pour liquid over bread and cheese. Prepare night before serving. Refrigerate; cover baking dish. Bake at 350 degrees for 1 hour uncovered. Place baking dish on cookie sheet because soufflé may bubble over. Serves 8 to 10.

Matthew 25:35 – "For I was hungry and you gave me something to eat; I was thirsty and you gave me something to drink; I was a stranger and you invited me in."

MAY 1970 – IMMANUEL'S MOTHER OF THE YEAR
TREVA GRAF

A presentation now
To Immanuel's Mother of the Year.
A very proud and happy moment
And the moment is almost here.

Our mother is a sweetheart
In each and every way.
You always see her with a smile
Each and every day.

Time is never on her hands;
She's always on the go
Doing things for others
As Immanuel's ladies know.

She's been a member of Immanuel
Since January of '54,
A Sunday School and church attender
And during the week a lot more.

Immanuel's Aid Society
Was a busy part of her life.
All this she did and still had time
To be the perfect mother and wife.

The National Lutheran Home
Has always been on her list,
Collecting dues and planning trips
And visitations never missed.

As a L.C.W. member,
The kitchen is her call,
Planning, preparing and serving
From winter until fall.

Canning or preserving,
Call it what you may,
She is in the kitchen working
At the very first break of day.

Hundreds and hundreds of jars of food
Ready for Washington, D. C.
And without her supervision,
Harvest Home Sunday could not succeed.

Of all the jars of tomatoes
That this lady had helped to can,
Would you believe it's the one food
That she positively can't stand.

At the mention of a public sale,
She lights like a Christmas tree.
She and her ladies make way for the kitchen
And start on their baking spree.

Three children has this mother
And seven grandchildren, too.
And since the year of '61,
Five great grandchildren have made their debut.

You must have some idea
Who this wonderful mother must be.
She always has the giggles
And a very find Christian is she.

May God bless and guide her
As she continues along her motherly path,
And give good health and happiness
To our own Mrs. Treva Graf.

FROM THE KITCHEN OF: TREVA GRAF
RECIPE FOR: Vanilla Refrigerator Cookies
INGREDIENTS: ½ cup shortening
1 cup sugar
1 egg, beaten
1 tsp. vanilla
1½ cups sifted flour
½ tsp. soda
½ tsp. salt

Cream shortening; gradually add sugar. Cream until mixture is light and fluffy. Add egg and vanilla. Mix Well. Sift together flour, soda and salt. Gradually add to mixture. Beat after each addition. Shape in a roll about 1-3/4" in diameter. Wrap in wax paper; chill. Slice ⅛" thick. Bake on cookie sheet in 375 degree over for 7-10 minutes. Makes 6 dozen.

Luke 10:8: "When you enter a town and are welcomed, eat what is set before you."

MAY 1971 IMMANUEL'S MOTHER OF THE YEAR
SUSAN "TOOTIE" CROFT

Mother's Day is here again
And a special one we honor.
Her worthiness for this tribute
Is one we need not ponder.

1914 was the year
That she became a mother.
A darling baby girl was born
And to her there was no other.

Sixteen years went by
And another daughter was born.
Little did they know
That a nurses cap would be worn.

A mother, yes,
And dedicated, too,
Because now she is grandma
To her grandchildren which number two.

Besides a wonderful mother and grandma
And a wonderful friend, also,
She's a wonderful wife and homemaker
As her hubby certainly knows.

In just a few days,
May 30th to be exact,
They will celebrate their 41st year
Since they signed their marriage contract.

IMMANUEL EVANGELICAL LUTHERAN CHURCH

Can you imagine 41 years
Of delicious sticky buns
Because our mother is a baker
And she rises with the sun.

"Ladies, ladies, in the kitchen,
We must begin at 5:00."
This cook believes in starting early
If the dough is expected to rise.

Communion has a special meaning
Several times a year
When this mother bakes the bread
That is brought to the altar here.

Since she and hubby joined us
In the year 1954,
She's been a busy and active lady
And nothing has been a chore.

Missionary Society
And Aid Society, too,
Were among early organizations
She was dedicated to.

Now she's a faithful member
In our L.C.W. here.
You will find her in the kitchen
With pies and doughnuts near.

She realizes the necessity
For our Daily Vacation Church School.
She and hubby serve refreshments
While others teach the Christian Rule.

Our honored lady gardens
And flowers are a must.
I wonder if her color of blue
Is a part of the skies surplus?

An early bird she certainly is
Along with her husband, too,
Because being an hour ahead of time
Is better than an hour overdue.

As her moment of birth came
In October of 1895,
May of 1971 brings
Another big moment about to arrive.

This lady has a nickname,
As Mr. Benjie knows,
Susan is her first name
But "Tootie" kneads the dough.

We now give honor
To Immanuel's Mother of the Year.
Yes, Mrs. Benjamin Croft,
Your big moment is now here.

May God Bless You
Each and every day
And bring you happiness and good health,
For this we earnestly pray.

FROM THE KITCHEN OF: Susan "Tootie" Croft
RECIPE FOR: Pepper Relish
INGREDIENTS: 12 red peppers
                12 green peppers
                12 small onions
                3 tsp. salt
                3 cups vinegar
                3 cups sugar

Grind peppers and onions. Pour boiling water over. Let stand 15 minutes. Squeeze all water out. Cook 35-40 minutes and jar. "I dilute with vinegar. If it's too sour, then I still add more sugar. I make it taste good."

FROM THE KITCHEN OF: Susan "Tootie" Croft
RECIPE FOR: Pumpkin Custard Pie
INGREDIENTS: 1½ cups pumpkin
                2 eggs
                1½ cups milk
                1½ tbsp. Flour
                ⅔ cup sugar
                ½ tsp. salt
                ½ tsp. cinnamon

Combine all ingredients. Pour into unbaked pie shell in 10" deep dish pie pan. Bake at 350 degrees for 45 minutes (until knife inserted in center comes out clean).

Psalm 34:8 – "Taste and see that the Lord is good; blessed is the man who takes refuge in him."

IMMANUEL EVANGELICAL LUTHERAN CHURCH

MAY 1972 – IMMANUEL'S MOTHER OF THE YEAR
MARTHA RILEY

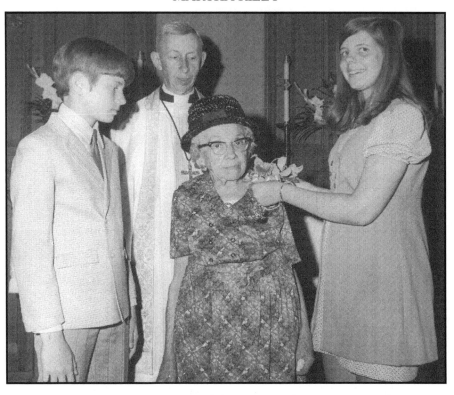

The month is May
And the year is '72.
Immanuel's Mother of the Year
Is about to make her debut.

Her life began
In September – 1884
And from that moment on
God shared each day a little more.

A bicycle ride for our mother
Used to be a real treat.
This was a favorite sport
Pedaling leisurely down the street.

Brother Dan must bring back memories
The day she stuck butter in his face.
The fact that he didn't like butter
Hurt more when she was put in her place.

This lady has learned many lessons
One of which goes something like this:
People papering walls on ironing boards
Break knees and must be dismissed.

Our very special lady
Had a courtship of our years,
But five years later was widowed,
Yet his memory she still holds dear.

SEASONED WITH RHYMES AND A PINCH OF THYME

A son was born in 1905
And a daughter in 1907,
But eight months thereafter,
Her daughter met God in Heaven.

The cigar and uniform factories
Kept her quite busy indeed,
But she never neglected her son and home
Or her sewing or planting the seed.

A faithful member of Immanuel
This lady has certainly been.
If her seat is empty one morning,
We begin to inquire within.

The reason for her absence
Wouldn't be the car breaking down,
Because our lady has walked to church
All of her life from downtown.

Our mother is, of course, a good cook,
But pardon her if you will, please.
She will never serve you any dish
Consisting of that stuff called cheese.

She lives on South Main Street
And has for 57 years.
You can always find her quilting
Since this hobby brings lots of cheer.

Our mother had to check on her son
In order to keep him straight,
So she often walked to Immanuel
To make sure he didn't arrive late.

You see this mother's son
Was once in Immanuel's employ.
His loyalty and service as janitor
Was a sample of his training as a boy.

Her son, John, has always been her joy
Except one or two times that we know,
Like the day he wore her corset to school
And forgot the strings weren't to show.

The exciting moment is very near
To unfolding before all of you
The name of our honored Mother
To whom this presentation is due.

Mrs. Martha Riley
How truly deserving you are.
We mothers of Immanuel
Would choose you as our guiding star.

Your life has held happiness
And, of course, sorrow, too,
But your example of true faith
Will remain with us through and through.

We pray God will bless you
With years of happiness and good health.
Your life with Him and your family
Are all part of your riches and wealth.

God Bless you on your day
As our Mother of the Year.
A red rose is not enough
So an orchid must be presented here.

IMMANUEL EVANGELICAL LUTHERAN CHURCH

FROM THE KITCHEN OF: Kathryn Riley (granddaughter-in-law)
RECIPE FOR: Pineapple Salad Mold
INGREDIENTS: In saucepan on medium heat put in:
        1 pack lime Jell-O
        1 pack lemon Jell-O
        16 large marshmallows
        2 cups water

Stir it until marshmallows are melted. To this mixture add 1 large can of crushed pineapple and cool until starting to jell. Mix together 1 package Dream Whip (beaten) and 1 - 3 oz package cream cheese. Add to Jell-O mixture and pour into mold.

I Corinthians 10:31 – "Whether, therefore, ye eat or drink or whatsoever ye do, do all to the glory of God."

MAY 1973 - IMMANUEL'S MOTHER OF THE YEAR
NAOMI GRAF

"Mothering is necessary –
Grandmothering – a luxury of life."
This quoted saying
Fits our devoted mother, grandmother and wife.

Such a fine lady
Who is loved by family and friends.
Her sweet smile and warm personality
Produces a very pleasant blend.

Immanuel's Mother of '73
Now listens, watches and waits
For any little clue
Of her life which she can relate.

I wonder if she's wearing blue
Because she wears it well.
I know it wouldn't be purple
Because to this color she does rebel.

Summertime brings memories
Especially of yesteryear.
Raspberry ice cream at the Zumbruns
I think she'll remember quite clear.

Wintertime meant sledding parties
And oh what fun that was.
Zumbruns, Hershs and Leeses
Would enjoy these memories as much as she does.

23

IMMANUEL EVANGELICAL LUTHERAN CHURCH

She was born in the year 1892
In Glenville, PA.
And in the same town in 1914
She celebrated her wedding day.

Reverend William Erhart
Was there to tie the knot
And she and Eddie were chauffeured
With a horse and buggy trot.

Millers Station, Maryland,
Was their very first home,
And each time they moved
Their family had always grown.

Remember taffy pulling times
And the day you misplaced your ring.
You were sure you lost it outside
But on a nail near the door it did swing.

Our mother is a great cook
Of just about everything,
But those delicious sticky buns
We think are her special thing.

Pumpkin pie is usually a favorite
But one day her pie didn't entice.
She forgot to add the sugar
But never made that mistake twice.

She's been a member of Immanuel
For about fifty-five years
And a member of Aid Society and Missionary
Which she has always held dear.

Patting oysters at the fire hall,
Homemakers and Senior Citizens, too,
Are more of her social life
That she loves through and through.

She attends the Women's Bible Class
And never lets L.C.W. out of view.
Being busy in our kitchen
Is a love that grew and grew.

She mixes the dough early;
The ladies peel apples and chat as they sit.
And she says, "Here we go again."
"Why do we do it?"

She has a date the 1st Tuesday of the month
And the time is 9:15.
Her Faith Group of L.C.W.
Makes sure she's on the scene.

When we arrive at her residence
(And that's Locust Street, you see,)
She'll always say "Now you girls
Shouldn't have to bother with me."

Speaking of Locust Street
She loves carnival time
When she looks forward to seeing her friends
And enjoys the excitement she finds.

Dorothy Naomi was her first born
And also her namesake, you see,
Then Lawrence Edward in 1920
And soon Glenice Genevieve.

Allen Leroy, known as Buddy,
Was the last child to be born;
Then making a family of six
And their very own home to adorn.

Our mother is a grandmother
And the total comes to four.
Patty, Douglas, Kim and Kelly
Are surely to be her adored.

Her twin granddaughters are so special –
Kim and Kelly Loats.
A good reason for a trip to Ohio
In June, we do denote.

A funny coincidence happened
Just the other day
When she wore an artificial orchid
And this she had to say.

"I'll never have a real orchid
Not an old woman like me,"
So today becomes a first
For our Mother of '73.

Well have you guessed
Just who she must be?
I'm sure you have
And so deserving, don't you agree?

God has been good to Immanuel
For sharing her with us.
We pray she continues with years of happiness,
Good health and always in God's trust.

So to a very special Mother
I announce in her behalf
That Immanuel's Mother of the Year
Is our own Naomi Graf.

FROM THE KITCHEN OF: Naomi Graf
RECIPE FOR: Old-Fashioned Molasses Ginger Cakes
INGREDIENTS: 1 gold label pt. bottle Brer Rabbit molasses
1 cup lard, just softened
1 cup sugar
1 cup thick sour milk or hot water
1 tbsp. baking soda
1 tsp. alum, dissolved in a little hot water
1 tsp. ginger
1½ tsp. cinnamon
5½ to 6 cups Pillsbury flour

Sift spices with flour. Cream molasses, lard and sugar together. Add sour milk and flour mixture alternately. Set in refrigerator for an hour or so to stiffen and cool dough. Roll on cloth sprinkled with flour and rolling pin covered with cloth. Cut thick. Sprinkle with sugar. Bake on slightly greased cookie sheet at 375 degrees. Watch closely; they burn easily. Makes approximately 4-1/2 dozen.

FROM THE KITCHEN OF: Naomi Graf
RECIPE FOR: Lemon Sponge Pie
INGREDIENTS: 2 tbsp. butter
1 cup sugar
2 tbsp. flour
Rind and juice of 1 lemon
2 eggs separated

1 cup milk

Cream butter and sugar; add flour. Add rind and juice of lemon. Add egg yolks and milk. Beat egg whites until frothy and add last. Bake at 350 degrees for 30 to 45 minutes in unbaked 9-inch pie crust.

FROM THE KITCHEN OF: Naomi Graf
RECIPE FOR : Chocolate Marshmallow Cookies
INGREDIENTS: ½ cup margarine
                 ½ cup sugar
                 1 egg
                 1 tsp. vanilla
                 ¼ cup milk
                 1¾ cup flour
                 ½ tsp. baking soda
                 ½ tsp. salt
                 ½ cup baking cocoa
                 24 marshmallows

Cream margarine and sugar. Add egg, milk and vanilla and mix. Add flour, baking soda, salt and cocoa. Heat oven to 350 degrees. Grease baking sheet. Drop dough by teaspoonful. Bake for 8 minutes. Remove from oven and IMMEDIATELY press ½ marshmallow (cut-side down) onto each cookie. Return to oven for 2 minutes. Cool.

Frost cooled cookies with: 3 cups confectioners sugar
                             4 tbsp. Baking cocoa
                             ⅛ tsp. salt
                             4 tsp. margarine
                             4 tbsp. cream

Proverbs 30:8 – "Keep falsehood and lies far from me; give me neither poverty not riches, but give me only my daily bread."

MAY 1974 – IMMANUEL'S MOTHER OF THE YEAR
KATIE WENTZ

I'm going to begin this presentation
In a very special way,
Not only to be different
But because it's a very special day.

So – "Roses are red,
Violets are blue,"
Immanuel's Mother of the Year
Is about to have a dream come true.

Why the roses and violets?
That's very easy to explain.
Her talent as a "green thumb"
Leads to her well known fame.

Our mother has many talents –
Gardening and quilting being just a few.
Crocheting afghans is a favorite
And she has made well over twenty-two.

This lady couldn't imagine
Throwing egg cartons away;
To her they are just as important
As the eggs – but in a different way.

She creates lovely flowers
By cutting the carton here and there.
She recently donated to Senior Citizens
Her centerpiece made with tender loving care.

27

IMMANUEL EVANGELICAL LUTHERAN CHURCH

Speaking of Senior Citizens,
She does double duty here.
She's not only a member in Manchester
Because Hampstead is also near.

Our mother loves to travel
Either by car, boat or train,
But her love for travel subsides
When you mention going by plane.

Our very lovely mother
Glows in the color of blue.
The accent to her hair and eyes
Shows why it's her favorite, too.

She and her husband
Came to Immanuel in 1952.
They generously provided the heating system
To our educational building when new.

The first Wednesday of each month
Her Sarah L.C.W. meets.
When oysters need to be patted and fried,
She's right there finding it a treat.

She was a member of the Aid Society
And Missionary, too.
She's in the Ladies Bible Class
And regular attendance is nothing new.

If each of us were as faithful
In attending church and meetings
There would be no need for worry
Or unnecessary pleadings.

Not only is she generous
In donating her services and time,
But also in presenting our sound system Helping to
project sermons, business and rhyme.

Triple Valley Homemakers
Is lucky to have her, too.
By sharing ideas and experiences
Makes her a special homemaker through.

Her home brings special memories
To leaguers, classes and such.
Along with her gracious hospitality,
Her bowling alley has been enjoyed very much.

Our mother has six children:
Kathryn, Miriam and George,
Mary Ellen, Ruth and Reba,
And fourteen grandchildren she adores.

Christian and Amy
Are very important, too.
They made her a great grandmother
And again her family grew.

Eighty-four years young on January 11th
Was our Mother of the Year.
March 21, 1914, another important day
When Spencer Wentz became her career.

We are honored at Immanuel
In his memory to be able to share
The "Reredos" his wife presented
For his dedication, which Immanuel is well aware.

Have you guessed our Mother of Immanuel?
Well, these facts wouldn't make much sense
If Immanuel's Mother of the Year
Was anyone but our own Katie Wentz.

She will always belong to Immanuel
Because of her thoughtfulness and concern.
Her example of a true Christian
Is one from which we can learn.

28

May God bless you, Mrs. Wentz
On this big day and for many more.
Our prayers are for happiness and good health
To Immanuel's Mother of the Year for 1974.

FROM THE KITCHEN OF: Katie Wentz
RECIPE FOR: Pennsylvania Dutch Salad Dressing
INGREDIENTS: 3 eggs
1 cup water
1/3-1/2 cup vinegar (to taste)
1½ cups sugar
1½ tbsp. cornstarch
½ tsp. salt

Beat eggs. Add water and vinegar. Combine sugar, cornstarch and salt. Add to egg mixture. Cook, stirring constantly until thickened. Cool to serve. Makes 3 cups. Dressing keeps in refrigerator 3 weeks. Serve dressing over broken lettuce, fried bacon pieces and chopped hard-cooked eggs.

1 Corinthians 10:17 – "Because there is one loaf, we, who are many are one body, for we all partake of the one loaf."

IMMANUEL EVANGELICAL LUTHERAN CHURCH

MAY 1975 – IMMANUEL'S MOTHER OF THE YEAR
BESSIE MILLER

A lovely face;
A beautiful smile;
A warm and loving heart
That has reached many a mile.

That's short but sweet description
Of our Mother of the Year,
But her busy and active life
Is as long as she is dear.

Her love has reached out
Both far and wide
And as a wife, mother and friend,
She's always been at their side.

God has always been the first
And she served Him in many ways.
Twenty-five years on the Adult Choir;
As an Alto she sang praise.

She is a faithful member
Of Immanuel Lutheran Church
Most Sundays she picks a backseat pew
If for her you wish to search.

A Sunday School Teacher she surely is
And has been for 54 years.
Teaching, singing and playing songs
And helping to wipe little tears.

Church suppers were always exciting
And she collected money at the door.
Now with the Father & Son Banquet,
Frying oysters is fun galore.

Aid Society and Missionary
Kept her quite busy then.
Now Ruth L.C.W. Group
Knows on whom they can depend.

Her church has meant so much to her
And she carried this right through
Because her example of a true Christian
In her precious family grew.

Her family never lacked her love
Because she was always there
Whether it be at home or operettas
And a missed Eisteddfod was very rare.

Sewing costumes or a winter coat
Was a simple task for our mother.
But her daughter tells me her doll clothes
Could have been made by no other.

A special costume remembered
By her daughter when in first grade
Was a bridal gown and veil
For a Tom Thumb wedding it was made.

And then there was a special dress
So fluffy and so pink.
A bonnet matched the outfit
Which made the boy dolls wink.

Another memory of a Mother's love
Took place many winters ago
When she pulled her children to school on a sled
Because of sidewalks covered with ice and snow.

Lovely Easter Gardens;
Beautiful Christmas Trees;
Childhood birthday parties;
And homemade ice cream and cake to please.

Now, many years later,
Her granddaughter enjoys all this,
Including grandmother attending her programs
For this she couldn't miss.

Now I haven't named her family
Because I have more to tell.
I want to save them all for last –
Just before we break the spell.

We've shared her love with her family
But her love reaches out once more
To her friends and her community
Which she certainly loves and adores.

She is a member of Rebekah Lodge
And a past Noble Grand.
A Fire Company Auxiliary member
And at suppers she always lends a hand.

Her favorite food is turkey
And strawberries certainly please.
I'm sure being a Manchester Homemaker
Finds her entertaining with ease.

She served her community as well
As writer for the Hanover Evening Sun.
She retired with 43 years of service
Commended on a job well done.

Retirement isn't fitting
For an active lady like this,
So now President of Senior Citizens
There isn't a meeting that she can miss.

When she isn't attending meetings,
She crochets, knits and sews,
Gardens, reads, plays piano;
Just enjoying her life with a glow.

Yes, you've passed her in the hallway
Or sat next to her in the pew
And if you noticed very carefully
She was probably wearing blue.

Our Mother was born on July 27th
In the year 1899
And since that time has cherished
Every moment of God's given time.

They raised two children together,
Paul F. Miller and Mildred McGrew.
They enjoyed their granddaughter, Jeanne,
And their son-in-law, John McGrew.

I've mentioned now her love has spread
From God – to family – to friends,
But I saved a very special love
Which only she can comprehend.

Immanuel's Mother of the Year
Has surely earned this day
And we wish for her the best to come
In every possible way.

On June 2, 1917
It was Harvey Miller she wed.
Together their life was filled with bliss
Until into God's hands he was led.

Yes, Mrs. Bessie Miller,
You're our Mother of the Year
And we pray for you God's Blessings
As each new day appears.

Won't you come before us now
So we can honor you.
Your family and friends of Immanuel
Wait as you make your debut.

FROM THE KITCHEN OF: Bessie Miller
RECIPE FOR: Walnut Kisses
INGREDIENTS: 3 large egg whites in cold bowl
½ lb 4X sugar
Cream of tartar that lays on end of knife
1 cup walnuts

Beat egg whites until stiff; add sugar gradually. Beat long and hard. Add cream of tartar, then nuts. Grease pans. Drop small amounts on sheet pan. Bake real slow in 250 degree oven. Return batter to refrigerator between each usage.

1 Samuel 25:6 – "Say to him: 'Long life to you. Good health to you and your household and good health to all that is yours."

MAY 1976 – IMMANUEL'S MOTHER OF THE YEAR
MYRTLE BERWAGER

Have you ever met an angel
Not necessarily dressed in white
But one that loves and cares for all
And pleases God with all that is right?

I have, and she lives in Manchester
And has for fifty-five years.
She is a member of Immanuel
And she is our Mother of the Year.

Let's go back a little ways,
Perhaps 86 years ago
In March of 1890
When she was rocked to and fro.

She recalls being punished
When skipping and jumping from her swing
And when she called her father "Archie,"
She recalls a few painful stings.

She worked for her father
In his saloon as chambermaid.
Beer was okayed for consumption
But no soft drinks and this she obeyed.

She studied at Peabody Conservatory
And her training was Immanuel's gain
Because she became our first organist
And led the congregation through many refrains.

IMMANUEL EVANGELICAL LUTHERAN CHURCH

Many times she can recall
When it became so cold in the church,
She practiced wearing boots and gloves
And finding the right chord became a search.

Unusual things are known to happen
On many a wedding day,
But would you get married at 5:30 a.m.?
Our Mother did with no delay.

They had to catch the train
From Maple Grove that day
To take them on their honeymoon
Down Alexandria, Virginia way.

They rode in style to the station
That 7th day of May
In a surrey with a fringe on top –
Just like a fairy-tale wedding day.

Now fairy-tale weddings don't happen
But this one was as real as could be
And has lasted for 63 years
Where love and devotion has flowed free.

She is a charter member of Homemakers
And a member of the Sunshine Club, too.
Ladies Aid Society brings back memories
And the Hospital Auxiliary, just to name a few.

But do you know what her children remember?
Not the clubs she served so faithful and so true,
But the fact that she was a dedicated homemaker
And was always there for them to come home to.

Her children have expressed this to me
As their feelings overflowed
About their precious mother
And the seeds of guidance she sowed.

She was and is a wonderful nurse
And has cared for many folks.
Relatives received her devoted care
And nothing too strenuous to provoke.

Three square meals a day
And as a family their meals were shared.
A mom with super patience
And a cook that couldn't be spared.

You haven't tasted potato soup
Until you have eaten hers.
Her daughter, Mary, does her best
But it's "Ma Ma's" the grandchildren prefer.

Ice cream taffy was a treat
And not just at home.
It was sold at suppers for a penny a piece
And just as sweet as honeycomb.

Some days when attending Peabody
Our mother had a choice for lunch -
A slice of strawberry shortcake
Or a delicious pickle to munch.

I know what I would have chosen
But she wouldn't have agreed.
She chose the pickle –
A nutritional choice, indeed.

Speaking of pickles brings memories
To her children on their birthdays.
This was a Baltimore shopping trip
By cattle truck and street car one way.

From Monroe Street they went downtown
And Lexington Market completed their day.
The bus ride home included
Pickles, braunschweiger and cracker buffet.

SEASONED WITH RHYMES AND A PINCH OF THYME

Her children remember her thriftiness
And the many clothes she made.
Even her own and hubby's shirts –
The treadle machine more than repaid.

Dad was the head of the household
And strict discipline was in line.
Both parents always agreed
When discipline rules were defined.

Christmas times were precious
With family traditions portrayed
And their special Christmas garden
Which was creatively handmade.

Around the pot belly stove
The family gathered on Saturday night.
Our mother appeared with her apples
And slices were eaten left and right.

Remember when your son was small
He anxiously called for you one day.
"Richard, what do you want?"
"I just want to kiss you!" his little voice did say.

Some favorites of our mother
Is her lovely color of blue.
She has quite a sweet tooth
But loves those parsnips, too.

We all have unusual habits
And our mother is of the same race.
When visiting she always leaves her purse
Containing a hanky, just in case.

She still loves to play the organ
And her piano, too,
Remembering that she made the noise
When silent movies were to view.

She sees beauty in everything
And even captures God's rain.
Her lovely flowers flourish
On rain water and green thumb pain.

At 86 years of age
She passes every test
From cooking to flowers to nursing
And her penmanship is one of the best.

Her church is very dear to her
And she keeps abreast of activities here.
If her daughter, Julia, forgets a bulletin,
She calls for delivery from anyone near.

Our mother has shared a very rich life
With Emory, her husband, so dear.
And her three adoring children,
Julia, Mary and Richard, all remain near.

This isn't all the family
Because four grandchildren have been reared,
And since God's story is of creation,
Four great grandchildren have appeared

This lovely mother has lived an example
Of what family life should be.
I hope you've been moved by her story –
I know she's made an impression on me.

Mrs. Myrtle Berwager,
Today you reign as our Mother of the Year
And what a special tribute
Since this is our Bicentennial Year.

Your story unfolds lots of history
And old fashioned traditions, as well.
If each of us could preserve just one,
We, too, would have a lovely story to tell.

Immanuel's prayers for you and your family
Are more and more of the same.
May you always find the beauty with God
That shines in you today as you reign.

FROM THE KITCHEN OF: Myrtle Berwager
RECIPE FOR: Shoo Fly Pie
INGREDIENTS: ¾ cup flour
½ cup firmly packed brown sugar
½ tsp. each of cinnamon, cloves, ginger & nutmeg
¼ tsp. salt
2 tbsp. Shortening
½ cup molasses
¾ cup boiling water
1½ tsp. baking soda
1 egg well beaten

Mix above and pour into pie crust. Bake 450 degrees for ten minutes and then reduce temperature to 350 degrees for 20 more minutes.

FROM THE KITCHEN OF: Myrtle Berwager
RECIPE FOR: Molasses Taffy
INGREDIENTS: 2 cups baking molasses
1 cup sugar
⅓ cup water
1 tbsp. Vinegar
2 tbsp. Butter

Fry ingredients in water. When crackly, remove from fire. Add a pinch of baking soda before pouring onto platter. Pull together until cool enough to handle. Stretch mixture and form into rope. Cut into pieces.

Psalm 136: 25-26- "He gives food to every living thing. His faithful love endures forever. Give thanks to the God of heaven. His faithful love endures forever."

MAY 1977 – IMMANUEL'S MOTHER OF THE YEAR
NAOMI SNYDER

If I could be an artist
Just for this special day,
I would announce Immanuel's Mother
In a very colorful way.

I'd use the largest canvas
That a sturdy easel would hold
And my palette would be filled
With every color that you could behold.

The reason for this being
Because of her colorful life
With busy years of activities
As citizen, homemaker, mother and wife.

I'd begin with a dab of pink
For that little girl and precious baby,
Swirling my brush until a rose is formed
For a very special lady.

Our mother was born on Mother's Day
May 7, 1909.
A special lady was her mother
And a more appropriate gift you couldn't find.

Eddie and Annie had a terrible time
Deciding on a name.
Everyone from grandfather to uncles
Turned this decision into a game.

IMMANUEL EVANGELICAL LUTHERAN CHURCH

Alas, the best source was researched
To give identity to our mother.
Her first name came from the Bible
And Grandmother Burgoon provided the other.

She was born on Grandfather Keck's farm
Just outside of our town;
Moving next to 206 South Main
And since '73, in Pennsylvania she can be found.

She loved to visit her aunts
Who resided in Hanover, P.A.,
But was never ready to go home
And she always begged to stay.

Now my brush finds yellow and orange
Because busy and vivacious were school days.
Her classmates loved her personality –
Always happy and helping out in any way.

But, being happy can get out of hand
And this happened to her one day
When she was sent home from school
Because her giggles got carried away.

She was a member of the Glee Club
And excelled in sports and dramatics.
Her fabulous job in "Ruth in a Rush"
Made her senior year quite climactic.

She played the leading role
As "Ruth" in this smashing hit;
Also "Safety First"
Brought out her humor and wit.

"Great oaks from little acorns grow"
Was her motto she threw back
When they called her "Peck, the runt of the class,"
So a sense of humor she didn't lack.

Manchester School's first yearbook
Had our mother on their staff.
She was the official Joke Editor –
The perfect source to make them laugh.

But laughing turned to tears
As Manchester's first graduation came near.
Naomi uttered her favorite words
Appropriately saying, "Oh, my dear!"

And now some strokes of red
For her horizons were now brightened.
When attending Towson State Normal
Adventuresome and a little frightened.

My brush now touches a boyish blue
As I introduce her mate.
Their wedding day in 1929
Proved Milton was part of her fate.

Grace Lutheran Parsonage in Westminster
Was the wedding place that day.
Vallie Brilhart and Earl Warehime
Attended them with best wishes to convey.

And now a couple strokes of pink,
Blended with ruffles of white.
A precious baby girl arrived
And proved to be a pure delight.

Dessie Ann kept Mother busy
Especially with her love for sewing.
There was PTA and Homeroom Mother
And her daughter's needs continued growing.

And now it's her daughter's wedding.
Let's use rainbow shades and a touch of blue.
Now after years of being three,
A son-in-law comes into view.

38

SEASONED WITH RHYMES AND A PINCH OF THYME

David joined the family
In November of 1948
And with his wife and in-laws
Created close ties that just don't break.

Immanuel has had her as a member
Since May of 1925
Giving us her time and devotion
Along with her vim, vigor and drive.

For many years she was a teacher
In Immanuel's Sunday School
And Bible School was also a part
Of her teaching the Golden Rule.

Pastels must be blended here
As Children's Day drew near.
Directing recitations and songs,
Brought her delight for many a year.

Because of her leadership ability
And such a hard worker at heart,
She always held an office
In any organization where she was a part.

This included our Missionary Societies,
L.C.W. and Ladies Aid,
Rebecca Lodge and Fire Company Auxiliary
And with County Auxiliary she made the grade.

The Auxiliary's local talent play
Has always been a hit,
And mother and daughter have played many roles
Portraying seriousness and wit.

Splashes of green and red and black
Bring to mind a favorite food.
A slice of delicious watermelon
Puts her in the most satisfying mood.

As a cook she is just tops
And also enjoys entertaining.
But if it's vegetable soup she's serving,
She hopes there are leftovers remaining.

Knitting, crocheting and needlepoint
Are hobbies she really enjoys.
The attention she gives to her violets
Suggests another talent she employs.

Her daughter suggests if you have doubts
There is just one thing you need to do.
Ask at any greenhouse or yard goods store
And the owner will assure you.

Another splash of orange,
Along with a little black,
Because in her enthusiasm for sports,
There has never been a lack.

When baseball time approaches,
She's a Baltimore Oriole fan,
And saw them win the first World Series Pennant
As she cheered them from the stand.

She enjoys her TV serials
And "Another World" seems to be the best.
While watching her favorite Lawrence Welk show,
She does find time to relax and rest.

Thomas and Tabitha are her cats
And before them there were others.
You see she had many 'children'
Because she is a special mother.

Faith is her L.C.W. group
And the name fits her way of living.
Faith is her guiding light each day,
Receiving much but always giving.

And now a soft shade of lavender,
A bit of pink and some white.
A lovely orchid has emerged
And on our mother makes a lovely sight.

Immanuel, I've created a masterpiece
Of a mother with rich and colorful years,
And to think so many have been given to us;
We are so grateful to someone so dear.

May God's blessings always be upon her
As her horizons become brighter and wider.
Now, please greet my perfect model –
Naomi Mandella Snyder.

FROM THE KITCHEN OF: Naomi Snyder
RECIPE FOR: Macaroni Salad
INGREDIENTS: 1½ cups sugar
                 3 tbsp. Mustard
                 ½ pint mayonnaise
                 4 hard boiled eggs
                 ⅓ cup vinegar
                 ½ tsp. salt
                 4 pieces celery (cut fine)
                 2 carrots (grated)
                 1 lb. macaroni (cooked)

Mash egg yolks with mustard, add milk, sugar, mayonnaise, salt and vinegar. Pour over cold macaroni. Mix in chopped egg whites, celery and carrots. (Her daughter says this is the best macaroni salad she has ever tasted.)

Luke 15:23 – "And bring the fatted calf here and kill it and let us eat and be merry."

MAY 1978 – IMMANUEL'S MOTHER OF THE YEAR
MYRTLE BRILHART

A great poet once wrote in a few words
A part of our philosophy for living –
"Beauty is Truth and Truth is Beauty"
Was his concept of God's plan in giving.

Our mother has this beauty
Since she is stunning to behold
And the beauty she sees around her
Is the truth her paintings unfold..

Yes, Immanuel's Mother of the Year is an artist,
As her lovely home will tell,
Where she displays her many talents
And her paintings blend quite well.

In Manchester on August 28, 1896,
Our mother made her debut.
Howard and Anna treasured her days
As she struggled, blossomed, and grew.

Memories of the Sunshine Society
Should bring a smile her way.
Her sister-in-law remembers
That becoming a member was a very special day.

Reverend Lau conducted her confirmation
And 1913 was the year.
With five others in the class,
Her Christian roots were planted here.

41

The following year she made a step
From her days at Manchester School.
Along with Ruth Krumrine and Minnie Burgoon,
They set out to learn life's Golden Rule.

Eaton and Burnette Business School
Was a step in the right direction.
She traveled by train to Baltimore
To learn her skills to perfection.

Her experience in the working world
Took her here and there;
From an auto parts firm in Baltimore
To the excitement of New York and Times Square.

But of all the contacts in the business world
There was one that became part of her life –
The office of Commercial Credit Company
And later she became the Vice President's wife.

July 20, 1918 She and John set the date,
Traveling between New York and Rognel Heights
But returning to Manchester,
which was part of their fate.

During World War I
She found no excuse for a separation,
Because she went with John to Georgia
Accepting this as an extra long vacation.

Their marriage wouldn't have been complete
Nor had that magic of excitement
Without the blessed events
Of Gladden and John's enlightenment.

Immanuel has gained through her service
Since she taught Sunday School here,
And this will bring memories of her teacher,
Miss Sarah Trump, whose memory she holds dear.

She finds an interest in so many things,
Which keeps her young and vivacious.
Whether it be entertaining or a game of bridge,
As a hostess she is very gracious.

Her many talents and abilities
Provide a means in which to share,
And she does this with her homemakers –
Always open to new ideas with which she can
compare.

Rewarding and pleasant times are provided
At Senior Citizens and Grace's XYZ.
Her L.C.W. group is a favorite
So there's just no telling where this lady might be.

She's a member of an unknown group
That has not officially organized,
But the "Merry Widows" do exist
With good times among the seven from which they
are comprised.

Her time is her own
And she uses it well,
Along with family and friends,
Her grandsons think she's swell.

Billy and Brian have a special place
In their grandmother's busy life.
She's blessed with family, friends and good health
And has conquered years of sadness and strife.

Our mother is a celebrity
And many know her well
If they have dined in Ocean City
At the Stephen Decatur Hotel.

Until a few months ago
Her painting was part of the décor,
But the owners wanted it as part of their home
To be able to admire it even more.

She lives each day as a new beginning
And she is a lovely example to everyone.
Wouldn't our lives have more meaning
If each night we could say, "a day well done"?

Beauty can be a lovely sight
As we see in our Mother of the Year,
But the truth in what she really is
Radiates a beauty that family and friends hold dear.

She is God's way of saying
To each one of us
That our golden years are just the beginning
If in Him we forever resolve to trust.

We pray for many more years of good health
To our mother who has a big and generous heart.
Your example of beauty and truth
Is why we are honoring you, Myrtle Brilhart.

FROM THE KITCHEN OF: Catherine Brilhart (daughter-in-law)
RECIPE FOR: Green Pea Salad
INGREDIENTS: 16 oz. bag green peas, cooked
                Grated carrot
                Chopped celery
                Chopped onion (optional)
                Dressing: ¾ cup mayonnaise
                1 tbsp. Vinegar
                1 tbsp. Sugar

Mix green peas, carrots, celery and onion. Mix dressing ingredients. Add to salad and mix.

And the Lord God planted all sorts of trees in the garden, beautiful trees that produced delicious fruit. At the center of the garden, he placed the tree of life and the tree of knowledge of good and evil."

IMMANUEL EVANGELICAL LUTHERAN CHURCH

MAY 1979 – IMMANUEL'S MOTHER OF THE YEAR
HILDA HANN

Mother's Day at Immanuel
Is a very special time.
This day brings us back to basics
As we hold the role of mother as sublime.

Noble and grand are the proper words
To describe Immanuel's Mother of the Year.
Her delightful smile and personality
Has greeted us for 64 years.

Along with our mother's family
Are many others gathered today;
A sight that is very precious
As was true in many a yesterday.

Mother's Day draws us together
As was frequently done in the past,
But the pace of life which now exists
Saves sharing family ties sometimes for last.

But not for our mother
As you will soon hear and see.
Her family ties are very close
As God intended them to be.

My first vision of our mother
Is one which I am sure you will agree.
She has a smile for everybody
Regardless of who it might be.

SEASONED WITH RHYMES AND A PINCH OF THYME

Since joining Immanuel in 1915,
She has become one of its faithful pillars,
As well as a pillar for her hometown,
Having lived 60 years plus in Millers.

Our mother is the oldest of her family
And knows the hard work raising sisters and
brothers,
While at the same time going to school, which she
loved,
And helping on the farm because there were no
others.

She seldom misses a Sunday in church
Or attending her Women's Bible Class,
And when L.C.W. needs kitchen volunteers,
Our mother will volunteer rather than pass.

At 12:30 on the 1st Wednesday of each month
The Priscilla L.C.W. meets.
Our mother was their hostess in May
With lots of goodies and treats.

As hostess she shares ideas
Learned at homemakers meetings.
Having raised a family of four,
She's experienced when it comes to eating.

Her green thumb is superb
As her lovely flowers prove.
While onions and potatoes are on their way,
Planting the rest of her garden will keep her on the
move.

Does the name McGee ring a bell?
I bet to our mother it does.
Because back in her single days,
McGee was who she was.

And then on September 24, 1921,
Her life took on a new whirl.
At Grace Lutheran Church in Westminster,
She married a young fella named Earl.

Lineboro, Maryland was their first home
And then to Millers where they decided to unpack.
But after living in three different homes,
They finally settled beside the railroad track.

Besides being a homemaker
She worked in the canning and sewing factories,
too,
But our mother wanted more of a challenge
So she excelled as her four children grew.

Regina, Theron, Shirley and Janet
Grew through her patience and love,
And this she has shared with other generations
Eighteen grandchildren plus thirteen great while
pleasing her Father above.

Yes, she was born in 1899
On a farm near Mexico.
She remembers either walking to her destination
Or else horse and buggy was the next way to go.

I feel like calling our mother
Immanuel's Sweetheart of the Year.
Along with her sweetness she expresses humility
And her family and friends hold her dear.

Our mother has shared many happy times
As well as sorrowful ones,
But being the wonderful Christian that she is
Has made her an example for everyone.

So look around and find a lady
With a smile that makes you feel great.
She might be dressed in her color of blue
And beside her will most likely be her mate.

She will have her family around her
Or at least they are somewhere quite near,
And they all have an important message to convey
That might bring a very happy tear.

As we greet our mother this morning
We wish for her the best for many a year.
We pray that God will continue to bless her
And that her family and friends will always be near.

Her family thinks she is the greatest mom,
Wife and grandma, too;
And, her son-in-law said don't forget
She's the best mother-in-law, through and through.

The anticipating is rising
But our mother must now have a clue.
So to Immanuel's Mother of 1979,
Hilda Hann, we today honor you.

FROM THE KITCHEN OF: Hilda Hann
RECIPE FOR: Bread Pudding
INGREDIENTS:

- 5 slices bread
- 1 strip of butter
- ¾ cup sugar
- 1 can evaporated milk
- 1 tsp. vanilla
- 1 pinch salt
- 1 cup raisins or coconut (optional)
- 3 eggs

Cover bottom of 9 x 10 inch baking dish with bread. Pour one cup of boiling water over the bread; let stand. Beat egg, sugar, softened butter, vanilla and salt. Gradually blend in evaporated milk. But through bread with 2 knives. Pour creamed mixture over bread. Bake at 325 degrees for 30 to 40 minutes.

FROM THE KITCHEN OF: Hilda Hann
RECIPE FOR: Stewed Tomatoes
INGREDIENTS:

- 1 can tomatoes
- 1 tbsp. Cornstarch
- 1 tbsp. Butter
- 2 slices bread broken into pieces
- 1 small onion (optional)
- ½ cup sugar
- Dash of cinnamon

Cut tomatoes into small pieces and put in saucepan. Add other ingredients and cook until thickened.

Psalm 127:2 – "It is useless for you to work so hard from early morning until late at night anxiously working for food to eat, for God gives rest to his loved ones."

MAY 1980 – IMMANUEL'S MOTHER OF THE YEAR
GWENDOLYN SCHAEFFER

A song was written years ago
For this very special day
Entitled M-O-T-H-E-R,
Which honored her in a special way.

Today I would like to rewrite this song
Of poetry and rhyme
Not deviating from its originality
But personifying it for this appropriate time.

M – is for Immanuel's Mother
The first of a new decade,
May 11, 1980,
And she to be revealed in a poetic way.

O – is for her gift of organization
In all that she attempts to do
From that of being a wife and mother
To serving as her church and community grew.

T – is for always keeping in touch
With family, friends and events.
Soap operas inform her of society's change
And her interest in life merits published
comments.

H – is for a happy homemaker
And at home she ranks at the top.
Her devotions and talents in Triple Valley

IMMANUEL EVANGELICAL LUTHERAN CHURCH

Continually flow and never stop.
E – is for evangelical – the good news –
And this she strives to convey.
What she has reaped from Immanuel Evangelical
She faithfully lives by day after day.

R – is for radiance
As her sweet and friendly smile will show.
In a few minutes when you meet her
You will see her personality glow.

O – is for offering her service
Wherever the need may be,
At the Farm Museum, Friendship Bible Class,
Or in Senior Citizens sharing her vitality.

F – is for fried chicken,
Which must be a favorite food.
Gino's seems to serve the best
While her husband and sister help create the mood.

T – is for teacher
Both in public education and Sunday School.
Twenty-five years at Immanuel
Teaching six-year olds the Golden Rule.

H – is for her hobbies,
Which are numerous to mention.
Stamps, rocks, and Christmas wreaths
Are just a few to lessen any stress and tension.

E – is for education
And for our youth she sees a great demand.
Towson State is her alma mater
Having scored the highest mark in an entrance
exam.

Y – is for yearning to travel,
And she has been to almost every state.
She gives her husband all the credit
For supporting her yearning and being so great.

E – is for embarrassment in the tomato field,
But a funny story I'm sure she will confess.
As it rained on her acetate dress that day,
The harder it rained, the shorter the dress.

A – is for active,
Especially in Parent Teacher Associations.
Bazaars, conventions and workshops
Prove to be hard work and not vacations.

R – is for reporter
Of the Hampstead Record and Carroll County
Times.
Loving to read, write and debate
Helps her column's popularity as it climbs.

G – is for grandmother
And fifteen receive her dedication.
A gifted grandson was selected
For a Chesapeake Bay Foundation scientific
operation.

W – is for her wedding anniversary
And September 12th will be the date.
Forty-four years of wedded bliss
Both working side by side with their mate.

E - is for the Exceptional Center
Which she supports with sincere concern,
As well as the Carroll County Association for
Retarded Citizens
Providing opportunities for each member to learn.

N- is for nostalgia in remembering
When her hubby tried to teach her to drive.
As she hit the moving train with the new Model-T
He said, "I'll do the driving if this marriage is to
survive."

SEASONED WITH RHYMES AND A PINCH OF THYME

D – is for December 10th
The birth date of our Mother of the Year,
But the year has always been kept a secret
Even from family and friends whom she holds
dear.

However, I found out when she was born,
But I'm not about to tell
How or what I discovered
Since her secret has been preserved so well.

O – is for oyster suppers
And patting oysters was her pleasure.
Her tasty fried sweet potatoes
Were anticipated and enjoyed as a treasure.

L – is for love unlimited
For her husband, family and friends.
Her joy begins with the sun rise
And lasts as her last prayer and the sunset blends.

Y- is for the year 1947
When she joined Immanuel congregation.
Years following she joyously witnessed
Her four daughters confirmation.

N – is for nature,
Which shares a part of each busy day.
She loves gardening, flowers and plants
And her green thumb conditions in a special way.

S – is for Spicer,
Which was her maiden name.
Both parents are now deceased
But her first-born's name and her mother's are the
same.

C – is for her loving children
Of which there are four beautiful girls.
Myrtle, Elaine, Frances and Ruth
Bring back memories of lovely blonde curls.

H – is for Hampstead
Where her roots have been planted.
Her door is always open
And family and friends just take this for granted.

A – is for Algrude, her husband,
Of course, the one whom she adores.
She helped him in that tomato field
Until finally her daughters could help with the
chores.

E – is for everlasting
And this their marriage has been and will be.
Through love and mutual respect
Their ties will continue to bind instead of free.

F – is for family
Where her top priority rests.
Their get-togethers remain important
As they continue to create new family nests.

F – is for her faith in God
Which has comforted her through painful days.
Her devoted faith in Immanuel Lutheran
Has been our reward in many ways.

E – is for her eagerness
To look on to many good years of life.
We pray for her good health and happiness
While continuing to be a mother, grandmother and
wife.

R – is for revealing who she is
Unless you know through this song of rhyme.
M-O-T-H-E-R O-F T-H-E Y-E-A-R
G-W-E-N-D-O-L-Y-N S-C-H-A-E-F-F-E-R
Today we honor you at this time.

FROM THE KITCHEN OF: Gwendolyn Schaeffer
RECIPE FOR: Cherry Pudding
INGREDIENTS: 1 cup sifted flour
                 2 tsp. baking powder
                 ⅛ tsp. salt
                 1 egg
                 ½ cup milk
                 ½ cup sugar (Splenda can be substituted)
                 1 tbsp. Shortening
                 2/3 cup sour pitted cherries (or other fruit)
                 Sauce: 2/3 cup liquid (cherry juice and water)
                 ⅓ cup sugar

Sift together the flour, baking powder, and salt. Sprinkle over cherries. Mix together egg, milk, sugar and melted shortening. Add flour and cherries. Pour into greased 8-inch baking dish. Mix diluted cherry juice and sugar and pour over unbaked pudding. Bake in a moderate over (375 degrees) for 30 minutes. Hint: Mix berries or cherries with flour before mixing.

(Her daughter, Frances, says this cherry pudding was served a lot because they had several sour cherry trees on their property.)

FROM THE KITCHEN OF: Gwendolyn Schaeffer
RECIPE FOR: Old Fashioned Ginger Cookies
INGREDIENTS: 1 pint Brer Rabbit molasses
                 1 cup soft lard
                 1 cup sour milk or buttermilk
                 1 cup sugar
                 1 tbsp. ginger
                 1 tbsp. soda (dissolved in a little milk)
                 Flour – start with 6 cups flour. You need enough
                 flour to make a soft dough.

Mix the above ingredients. Roll on floured board to ¼ inch thick. Cut with large size glass or cutter. Place on cookie sheet about 1-1/2 inch apart. Bake at 375 degrees for 12 to 15 minutes.

Psalm 18:1 – "I love you Lord; you are my strength.

SEASONED WITH RHYMES AND A PINCH OF THYME

MAY 1981 – IMMANUEL'S MOTHER OF THE YEAR
RUTH ELIZABETH RILEY

We are born into this world alone
Not at our own discretion
Strange to faces, sounds and things
And in need of love and protection.

If, at our time of birth,
We enter with bat in hand,
We are assumed a rough and ready character –
A promising husband, father and all-around man.

But, when we make our debut
A pink bow is first to be seen,
Soon a lady of ruffles and lace,
A wife, mother and queen.

Today is that special time of year
We show honor to that queen.
Immanuel puts her in the limelight
As God's example, so she should be seen.

There are very special times
Immanuel's Mother will remember
Such as May 22, 1921,
When she became Immanuel's member.

Ladies Aid Society brings back memories
Of how The Lions Club loved them to cook.
They ate all the fried potatoes
Leaving none for those whose time and hard work
it took.

IMMANUEL EVANGELICAL LUTHERAN CHURCH

Her home is an example of caring
And in homemaking she excels.
She loves to cook for family
And she is creative here, as well.

Of all the delicacies she creates,
You will seldom find ones with cheese,
But when it comes to choosing her favorite,
It's homemade soup which seems to please.

Our mother has a love for beauty
And her flowers take first place,
As well as lovely handiwork
Where crocheted afghans leave just a trace.

Immanuel's Mother loves her friends
And cherishes warm summer nights
When neighbors gather for handiwork projects
Preparing to make someone's Christmas bright.

Every day has adventure
Especially when taking trips by bus.
This is a favorite pastime
Because, as the man says, they "leave the driving
to us."

In her Senior Citizens Club
She's eager to do her part.
For two years she baked monthly birthday cakes
Providing each a card with best wishes from her
heart.

In Nineteen Hundred and Seventy-Nine
The honor was hers alone
When selected Outstanding Senior Citizen
Well deserving this prestigious throne.

Serving her community
Is a priority on her list.
Eastern Star and Ladies Auxiliary
Are two she finds hard to resist.

Christmas has special meaning
To the children of her neighborhood.
She creates gifts for each one
As she spreads her love stemming through
motherhood.

Along with being a homemaker,
She has worked outside, as well.
The Manchester Pants Factory
Provided another source where she did excel.

Our mother has enjoyed a blissful marriage –
February 3, 1927 was the year.
She became a bride to John
As Reverend Rehmeyer tied the knot here.

As a wife she has been devoted
And her husband would testify to that.
She never needs to question where
He heads each morning for coffee and a chat.

She passed another requirement
For our Mother of the Year
When two sons were born to them
And have always remained near and dear.

Their sons have always been synchronized
Even when joining the armed forces.
When John married the 20th of October,
Danny said, "I do" the next day as if there were no
choices.

Five grandchildren have been their delight
And each year a special time comes their way.
On the Sunday after Christmas
The whole family is together for the day.

By this time I have given
Some very prominent hints,
But I'm sure to our mother
September 16, 1906 will surely convince.

She was born on the Gordon Farm
On the Fridinger Mill Road,
And Lena and Allen Lippy
Were the proud parents that were bestowed.

We are just as proud and happy,
As we know your family must be,
And we wish for you many years
Of health and happiness as God deems to agree.

Why should we wait any longer
To meet and honor Immanuel's Mother.
Ruth Elizabeth Riley,
Today you outshine each and every other.

Won't you come before us now
As an orchid waits presentation to you.
Immanuel's Mother of 1981 –
May God's blessings be constantly renewed.

FROM THE KITCHEN OF: Ruth Elizabeth Riley
RECIPE FOR: Pumpkin Pies (makes two pies)
INGREDIENTS: 1 cup sugar
                       2 cups mashed pumpkin
                       3 eggs
                       Salt
                       3 tbsp. Flour
                       3 cups milk
                       Spice

Mix all together and pour into two pie crusts unbaked. Heat over at 500 degrees. When crust is brown, reduce heat to 375 degrees for 45 minutes.

Psalm 9:2 – "I will praise you, Lord, with all my heart; I will declare all your wondrous deeds."

IMMANUEL EVANGELICAL LUTHERAN CHURCH

MAY 1982 – IMMANUEL'S MOTHER OF THE YEAR
BEATRICE CATHERINE YINGLING HULL

Our church is filled this morning
With God's families on this Mother's Day,
And so Immanuel wishes to all our moms
The very best on this 9th day of May.

Now Immanuel has had a tradition
To honor a Mother of the Year.
This year is no exception
So relax now, and lend me an ear.

Let's go back to our mother's childhood
When her mother was so special to her.
Her devotion grew in the years to come
Caring and nursing when poor health occurred.

Her childhood was very exciting
Along with two sisters and two brothers.
Our mother's love for them has remained
And that bond can be compared to no others.

They told me of a special Sunday
When she was dressed up for all to view
And on the way to church in the buggy
It upset and ruined her brand new white shoes.

Her precious baby brother,
Who had such beautiful, rosy, fat cheeks,
Always got such compliments
From all who came to take curious peeks.

SEASONED WITH RHYMES AND A PINCH OF THYME

Now our mother wanted the same attention
So one time she disappeared for a while,
But when she made her next appearance,
Her cheeks were stuffed with paper along with a
great big smile.

She gave them many anxious moments
Because of her love for height,
Especially when falling from the hayloft
And lying unconscious in their sight.

But Dr. Sherman came to the rescue
And pulled her through that day,
But soon after she climbed on top of the china
closet
Landing in the middle of a broken dish display.

Today she carries a scar of her childhood
When a sharp scythe fell on her arm.
With no hospitals in the area,
Her loving parents saved her and minimized the
alarm.

Her childhood included her husband-to-be.
However, at the time she was not aware.
They met during their school days
And we are sure it was love at first stare.

It happened in Royers Schoolhouse
But they really didn't know
That sticking tongues out at each other
Would make their friendship grow.

Years flew by but guess what happened.
Their wedding day arrived.
A '29 Ford Roadster left for Niagara Falls
And since 1933, a wonderful marriage has
survived.

Her younger sister cried that day
Seeing her in blue satin and lace.
She was almost like a mother
And now she would miss seeing her loving face.

Your sister-in-law remembers
When you both put mud clay on your face.
It hardened while you picked lima beans
And you stopped traffic all over the place.

A very special memory
Before the arrival of their baby carriage
Was walking barefoot in the stream
While experiencing the early years of marriage.

Their first home was with his mom and dad
For just about a year,
And then when made a gift of a horse,
The Shue Farm was where they began their career.

The Leese Farm was home for a while
And then the big day drew near
When they made the first down payment
On what has been home for 47 years.

1935 was the year
Their address was finalized,
And in 1938,
Farm help was realized.

On September 14, 1938,
Their helper made his début.
Pop wasted no time at all
In finding Donald something to do.

Don gave them lots of memories
Like falling out of an apple tree
And suffering a broken arm
While throwing apples at his brothers, you see.

IMMANUEL EVANGELICAL LUTHERAN CHURCH

And will she ever forget the day
Donald could not be found
Until from the chop chute in the barn
A small voice made a crying sound.

On October 26, 1941,
Richard Lee arrived.
His curls were the closet they came to their girl
But he showed them he could survive.

She loved to work with pretty curls
And one day she couldn't resist
To dress him up like a little girl
But his bow legs just didn't fit.

You have heard it said "we just made it,"
Well, they just did when Steve came to Mom and
Pop.
He came into the world in a hurry
And to this day he has yet to stop.

Our mother was almost assassinated
When a B-B gun shot her by mistake.
Steve had aimed at Richard
But he ducked in the nick of time sake.

He remembers delicious egg sandwiches
Being packed in his school lunch each day,
But one day bologna showed up
And he knew someone switched lunches that day.

Life was happy and busy
Everyone caught up in a whirl.
Babies, farming and chickens
And now hopefully expecting that baby girl.

Well, she was born in August
Of 1945
Her name was Charles Jesse,
And now a fourth son had arrived.

He wasn't any different
In making her life exciting,
But joined in the falls and broken arms
And was separated with the broom when all four
were fighting.

He remembers carrying his bucket
And picking strawberries with his mother
With memories of the treat in store
Since her strawberry shortcake was like no other.

A painful memory was when nine hornets
Made him their target for attack,
But there was always care and comfort with mom
As she immediately sucked the venom from his
painful back.

And then the year arrived
When they felt they could take a trip,
Leaving the boys for three days
To hold down a tightly run ship.

The first day Steve drank gasoline;
The second day Jesse was hit by a car;
The third day Richard was thrown from a horse,
But thankfully these memories left only scars.

Ask her and she will tell you
That the good times helped her get through
Such as little fists with bouquets of dandelions
Or bluebells from their five acre "Sea of Blue".

The aroma of doughnuts and warm apple pie
Was met by four boys returning from school.
Their feet couldn't move fast enough
To devour the goodies before they had a chance to
cool.

SEASONED WITH RHYMES AND A PINCH OF THYME

She was the family barber
For her sons and nephews, too,
But her husband never volunteered
Regardless of how long his hair grew.

Little pigs were often born
In the cold and wintry weather.
Our mother warmed them under the cookstove
Until they could all survive together.

Pot pie on cold Saturday mornings
Were welcomed by one and all.
After hours of cutting firewood,
She knew hungry appetites would be on call.

The experience of going to the river
With their dad was always a real winner,
Along with the anticipation on Sunday
Of their mother bringing them a fried chicken
dinner.

She always found something to make
From whatever was the "catch of the day".
Perhaps fried rabbit or squirrel pot pie
Or turtle soup as the "soup of the day."

Her nephew was their house guest
The day she served turtle soup.
After eating three hearty bowls she revealed her
recipe
At which time he hastily left the group.

She supported her boys in every way
Helping to organize Immanuel's Cub Pack.
Watching with pride as they advanced in scouting
Was an experience she wasn't about to lack.

Dick earned the Pro Deo Et Patria award,
The highest award the Lutheran Church gives to a
scout.
Steve served as Scout Master for 10 years
And grandson, Scott, earned his Eagle Award
without a doubt.

Running the boys to choir practice,
Trombone and cornet lessons, too.
Nothing was too much for our mother,
Always pleasing her family as they grew.

Boys grow fast,
As our mother surely knows,
And what helped them along
Were the weekly ten bread loaves.

Fried chicken and mashed potatoes
Have always been a specialty
Because of the 2,000 chickens
That were part of their growing family.

Peeps arrived in February;
Chickens grew fat for the platter;
Eggs were laid and gathered;
And a few cracks didn't matter.

When working, our mom didn't have to worry
Of the whereabouts of the youngest son.
He was confined in a bushel basket
Watching her tend her chickens until her work was
done.

Graduation days came
And it seemed just like yesterday
That the first school bag was bought
And she had waved them on their way.

IMMANUEL EVANGELICAL LUTHERAN CHURCH

Uncle Sam has a way of interfering
In a person's daily routine.
So, Donald was the first to join
The United States Marines.

"Anchors Away"
Was Dick's choice of songs.
The United States Navy
Was where he wanted to belong.

Steve shared the same feeling
And so to the sea he went,
But you better believe they soon headed home
As this is where weekends were spent.

Jesse followed big brother's footsteps
And for the Marines he gave three cheers,
But Jesse did something Don didn't do –
He brought home a wife as his souvenir.

Now even though she had no daughters,
Her friends have heard her to say
That where there are boys in the family,
You are sure to have daughters some day.

And that's just what happened
When her four boys tied the knot.
Her daughters-in-law came along
And the desire for a daughter was soon forgot.

August 26, 1912,
Our Mother of the Year was born
Never realizing in years to come
She would be helping Ralph plant corn.

Their skill in working with God's earth
Is one that many admire.
Her beautiful flowers and vegetables
Display her faith which her God did inspire.

Whether it be a rock garden
Or a piece of battered driftwood,
Her hands work the magic that is needed
Creating a masterpiece where the ordinary once
stood.

Regardless of what plant her daughters-in-law
Have left dry up and succumb,
She gently takes the last remains
And nurtures it back with her gentle green thumb.

She joined Immanuel Lutheran
In July of 1951
And has since been very active
In assisting everyone.

A past L.C.W. Group Leader
To the Hope Group she now belongs.
As an experienced Altar Committee member,
She's called on when things go wrong.

She arranges the lovely altar flowers
For chapel during Vacation Bible School.
Her good ideas for favors
L.C.W. gladly accepts as a rule.

Sunday School has been special to her,
Especially her Friendship Bible Class.
For many years she helped in the Nursery,
But remembers each one although many years
have passed.

Our Mother-Daughter Banquets,
Which is Immanuel's yearly highlight,
Was organized with our mother's help
Continuing since 1956 to everyone's delight.

58

SEASONED WITH RHYMES AND A PINCH OF THYME

Her friends are very special to her
As she certainly is to them.
The Hoffs and Ferriers share a special place
And as a traveling companion they think she's a
gem.

Her 60th birthday was celebrated
In Yellowstone National Park.
Willie and Hilda describe her excitement
Seeing a mouse in her new car and leaving his
mark.

Being a lover of nature
The geyser was to her a fascination.
Our mother was sure the devil was down there
Making that heat and steam for people's
devastation.

Grant and Edna share happy memories
Of their West Virginia scenic train ride.
When the girls almost missed the train
And they laughed as they ran until they cried.

Remember the excitement you caused
When visiting your son at Camp Lejune?
When word got out there were girls on the base,
You were surrounded by Marines very soon.

But the romance quickly ended
When asked why she was there.
Very meek and mild she answered,
"I'm here to find my son, somewhere."

At Chincoteague you loved the ocean
And as you watched the waves roll in,
Your friends never forgot your comment,
"How anybody cannot believe in God must be a
sin."

Today in sharing these memories,
I feel I have constructed a quilt;
One pieced with swatches of memories
From the life which our mother has built.

Quilting just happens to be a hobby,
And her granddaughters are always in mind,
As she makes sure each are remembered
With patches of memories in colors of every kind.

She secures her quilts with knots;
An example of her marriage vows;
Held tight and never broken;
Well constructed to weather all clouds.

There has seldom been a dull moment
In the married life she has known,
And now after 49 years of marriage,
She proudly observes how her family has grown.
She has now been blessed with grandchildren,
Four boys and five girls in all.
She brings to them that same love and concern
As their fathers many times recall.

Charles Jesse made up for the disappointment
When instead of a girl he was a boy
By presenting to her this past October
Twin girls to give her double joy.

Now it's BaBa and Pop Pop
And no greater grandparents could there be.
The grandchildren love the farm
Because of the loving foundation they see.

She has been the example to her daughters-in-law
Of what God expects a wife and mother to be.
Her patience in coping one day at a time
Is proven when she says, "This too shall pass,
you'll see".

Her memories will always be rich
As was the soil her husband worked to perfection.
And their four best crops have flourished
By fertilizing with love and correction.

Her favorite flower is the yellow rose
And I think it is time to present
Our gift from Immanuel Lutheran,
Which this bouquet represents.

Thanks and love go out to her
From her family and one and all.
We are so proud of you today,
BEATRICE CATHERINE YINGLING HULL.

FROM THE KITCHEN OF: Beatrice Catherine Yingling Hull
RECIPE FOR: Cucumber Salad
INGREDIENTS: 1 tbsp. mayonnaise
3 tbsp. Sugar
3 tbsp. Evaporated condensed milk
½ - 1 tsp salt
1 tbsp. Vinegar
1 large cucumber

Combine the first five ingredients. Slice cucumber into salt water. After soaking, squeeze out and add to the salad dressing.

FROM THE KITCHEN OF: Beatrice Catherine Yingling Hull
RECIPE FOR: Buttermilk Apple Pie
INGREDIENTS: 1 Unbaked pie crust
1 egg
1 cup sugar
1 cup buttermilk
2 tbsp. flour
Pinch of salt
½ Tsp. vanilla
1 pound Granny Smith apples (about 5)

Beat eggs lightly and add all other ingredients. Turn apples through the mixture. Pour into pie shell. Bake at 375 degrees for 30 minutes.

Remove and sprinkle topping of: ½ cup brown sugar, ⅓ cup flour, ¼ cup butter. Reduce over to 350 degrees and bake 15 more minutes. (Every Thanksgiving and/or Christmas, Chris Hull Manley and Scott Hull make sure this is served as one of their desserts.)

FROM THE KITCHEN OF: Beatrice Catherine Yingling Hull

RECIPE FOR: Pumpkin Squares
INGREDIENTS: 1 tbsp. Unflavored gelatin
                ¼ cup cold water
                1¼cup pumpkin
                3 eggs separated
                1 cup sugar
                Pinch of salt
                ½ tsp. cinnamon
                ½ cup milk

Soften gelatin in cold water. Set aside. Combine egg yolks, ½ cup sugar, salt, spices and milk. Cook in top of double boiler until mixture thickens (10-15 min.). Remove from heat and add gelatin and stir until dissolved. Cool. Beat egg whites, add remaining sugar and beat until thick and glossy. Fold into cooled mixture. Pour over crumbs. Chill and serve cut into squares. Garnish with whipped cream or cool whip.

Bottom Crumbs: 1 cup graham cracker crumbs
                  2 tbsp. Sugar
                  ⅓ cup margarine.

Mix and press in serving dish.

FROM THE KITCHEN OF: Beatrice Catherine Hull
RECIPE FOR: Seven-minute Icing
    INGREDIENTS: Place in a sauce pan and melt together. Barely
bring to   a boil.
                ¼ tsp. cream of tartar
                1 cup sugar
                ⅓ cup water
                1 tbsp. White Karo syrup

Beat until frothy but not stiff: 1 egg white. Put mixer on high speed, add melted ingredients in a slow stream. Add 1 tsp. vanilla and continue beating for at least 7 minutes. Beatrice would say, "If you want the telephone to ring, start making seven-minute icing."

Psalm 111:3 – "Majestic and glorious is your work. Your wise design endures forever."

IMMANUEL EVANGELICAL LUTHERAN CHURCH

MAY 1983 – IMMANUEL'S MOTHER OF THE YEAR
ETHEL VIOLA YINGLING MARKLE

Mother's Day is again upon us
This 8th day of May, 1983,
A day we hold in high esteem
For the dear one who held us on her knee.

Somewhere a newborn cry is heard,
And motherhood again expands,
A role with rewards insurmountable
As well as many daily demands.

Responsibility for a new life
Can produce anxiety and fear
Until we realize we are not alone,
But that our Father is always near.

Our mother has never forgotten
That her Father has always been near.
She has relied on him throughout her life
When times were hard and her husband was not
here.

She is God's example of motherhood
Even now that her family has grown.
The pattern God lays before all mothers
She has cut, fit and sewn.

Our mother was born at harvest time
When her mother was needed in the field.
Big sister pushed her across plowed ground
Where a hungry and fussy baby was revealed.

SEASONED WITH RHYMES AND A PINCH OF THYME

Old Bachman's Valley Road
Was the place of our Mother's birth.
To Grace and Ruth and our mother,
The Yingling farm became their salt of the earth.

Shades Schoolhouse was her first school
Where she had to walk two miles each day.
But if "Pop" and Ruth happened by,
The spring wagon took her the rest of the way.

Old Fort Schoolhouse was her next school,
And Miss Adda Trump taught her there.
One day our mother spilled her ink bottle
And left Grace's white dress the object of despair.

Remember the poem about "6 times 9"
Which you were to memorize and recite
In order to remember the answer
And learn your tables just right?

"So, I took my favorite Mary Ann
And called her '54'"
Now when the teacher asked, "6 times 9?"
She answered, "Mary Ann" and hoped for a
perfect score.

From Old Fort Schoolhouse to Manchester
With Gertrude Brilhart as her teacher,
Bringing the love of music into her life
And free piano lessons as a special feature.

Philip Royer was her 7th grade teacher
When attending Manchester School.
Because of double seats in the classroom,
Madeline Wolf shared in learning the Golden
Rule.

Operettas were a big event
During her high school years.
She participated with the gypsies
At Odd Fellas Hall I'm told by her peers.

At age 16 she joined Immanuel Lutheran,
And a hymn she sang that day
Was "Oh Happy Day, Oh Happy Day
When Jesus washed my sins away".

She graduated from Manchester Academy
With a class of only five,
And now fifty-five years later
This beautiful memory we today revive.

Now ready for the working world
She was employed at Woolworth's 5 and 10
Earning $8.50 for 52 hours a week
But this working girl now had her own money to
spend.

Then one day it happened;
A blind date with a ball player from Midway.
In his Chevy Roadster he drove his friend
To date Madeline, he would say.

But we know there was another reason,
And our mother can testify to that;
Four years later in 1937
John made a hit, but this time without his bat.

They were married in Immanuel
And Rev. Lewis Rehmeyer performed the
ceremony.
Madeline and Harry Smith stood for them
As they commenced their future in matrimony.

A honeymoon in Atlantic City,
Chauffeured by Madeline and Harry.
Two years later arrived a baby girl –
Peggy Cecile made their life exciting and merry.

A brand new white bungalow was built
On the corner of their farm.
New homes bring a new baby,
So, Douglas appeared with all his wit and charm.

IMMANUEL EVANGELICAL LUTHERAN CHURCH

And then Uncle Sam came to call;
He wanted John in the Seabees.
His wife and family moved back to the farm,
But after 19 months, he returned from the high
seas.

They were now together once more
But their family wasn't complete.
In October of 1948
Stanley produced the patter of more little feet.

Our mother is truly a homemaker
As she adds a touch of Pennsylvania Dutch.
Hog Maw, pot pie and chicken corn soup
And baking a cake every week, which John enjoys
very much.

She helps Doug during his tax season
And gives him her full dedication.
She has served on the Election Board
Since her father's resignation.

Life is quieter now
As their family has grown and relocated,
But their time together is so enjoyed
Soon being 46 years to be celebrated.

They have four grandchildren
And one great grandchild,
An adopted dog named "Freddie"
Who has blended into their new life style.

There isn't much she doesn't love doing:
Gardening, canning, quilting and reading,
Playing games, collecting stamps,
And where there are children, she will be leading.

Our mother began teaching Sunday School
At the age of 16 years,
And 55 years later
She is still preparing as each Sunday nears.

Her first class was 8-year olds –
Mary Rehmeyer was one of the members –
Known as the Primary and Junior Departments
And located in the social room, if you will
remember.

She was then moved to teach
Children who were 11 years old.
Among them was Henry Hoffman
And many of you, so we are told.

Our mother taught her class
Until she became a mother.
When her daughter was two years old,
She again returned to teach to many others.

She will remember the church parlor,
And believe me, so do I.
This was now her Sunday School room
Where many of us saw God's stories come alive.

She took only two leaves of absence
Since continuing in 1941;
Just time enough to raise a family
With the births of her two sons.

"Oh Who Can Make a Flower",
A song that I'll never forget.
"Jesus Loves Me, This I Know",
One you can hear her teaching today, yet.

Along with her devotion in teaching,
She has served our church in other ways,
Aid Society and Altar Guild,
Having led to L.C.W. which she enjoys today.

Our adult choir felt a loss
When she decided to retire.
A faithful alto member
Who sang 20 years on Immanuel's Choir.

64

She always thinks of others,
And never jumps to blame.
Like her mother, she never says an unkind word,
And has taught her children to do the same.

Lillie and Milton Yingling
Would be so proud to see
How dedicated their daughter has become
To her God and family.

Our mother loves all mankind,
And has a love for life.
She has served her church and family,
And has been a faithful and devoted wife.

Immanuel thanks her and salutes her
For all her effort and time that she shares
In teaching and serving in our church –
Just an example of how our Father truly cares.

Have you guessed who is our Mother of the Year?
It's the lady whose smile has a sparkle.
Let us prepare to greet her –
Our very dedicated Ethel Viola Yingling Markle.

FROM THE KITCHEN OF: Ethel Viola Yingling Markle
RECIPE FOR: Lima Bean Casserole
INGREDIENTS: 10 oz. lima beans
¼ cup reserved cooking liquid
4 slices bacon
½ cup chopped onion
¼ cup celery
¾ cup shredded Cheddar cheese
⅛ tsp. black pepper
Dash of Worcestershire sauce

Cook lima beans in lightly salted water. Reserve liquid. Fry bacon until crisp. Blot in paper towels and crumble. Drain bacon grease. In same pan sauté onion and celery. Add limas and reserved ¼ cup liquid, cheese, pepper, Worcestershire sauce and half of the crumbled bacon. Pour into greased 1 quart casserole dish. Sprinkle top with remaining bacon. Cover the dish and bake in 350 degree oven for 20 minutes. Remove the cover and bake another 5 minutes.

(Her daughter says Ethel was famous for taking this dish to every affair needing a covered dish. Of course, she made it with her own home-grown pole lima beans from her garden.)

FROM THE KITCHEN OF: Ethel Viola Yingling Markle
RECIPE FOR: Orange Kiss Me Cake
INGREDIENTS: 6 oz. frozen orange juice concentrate, thawed
2 cups flour

1 cup sugar
1 tsp. baking soda
1 tsp. salt
½ cup shortening
½ cup milk
2 eggs
1 cup raisins
⅓ cup chopped walnuts.

Combine ½ cup of orange juice concentrate with flour, sugar, baking soda, salt, shortening, milk and eggs in a large bowl. Blend at lowest speed on mixer for 30 seconds. Beat 3 minutes at medium speed. Stir in raisins and chopped walnuts. Pour batter into greased and floured 9 x 13 pan. Bake at 350 degrees for 40-45 minutes.

TOPPING: Drizzle remaining ¼ cup orange juice over warm cake. Combine and sprinkle over the top: ⅓ cup sugar, ¼ cup chopped walnuts, 1 tsp. cinnamon.

FROM THE KITCHEN OF: Ethel Viola Yingling Markle
RECIPE FOR: Soft Sugar Cakes (makes 4 – 5 dozen)
INGREDIENTS: ¾ cup shortening
2 cups sugar
2 eggs
½ tsp. salt
2 tsp. baking powder
1 cup buttermilk or thick sour milk
1 tsp. baking soda
½ tsp. cream of tartar
4 cups flour

In large mixing bowl cream shortening and sugar until fluffy. Add eggs, salt and baking powder. Beat until creamy. Mix milk, baking soda and cream of tartar in a 2-cup container. Add milk alternately with the flour mixture.

Drop batter by large spoonfuls onto greased cookie sheet. Sprinkle with sugar. Bake on upper rack in a 400 degree oven for 7 minutes. Cookies are done when no fingerprint can be made on top, and bottoms are lightly browned.

Matthew19:14 "But Jesus said, 'Let the children come to me, and do not hinder them; for to such belongs the kingdom of heaven.'"

MAY 1984 – IMMANUEL'S MOTHER OF THE YEAR
LOUISE WILHELM

May is that special month
When new beginnings come into bloom;
Flowers, trees, a new season,
And our life since Christ arose from the tomb.

The person who chose this special month
In which to celebrate Mother's Day
Must have felt the depth of God's love
Since life springs forth in every way.

Immanuel's Mother of 1984
Has spread love throughout her life.
Love is the bond of generations
Portrayed by our great grandmother, mother and wife.

It all began in Trenton
On the family farm
Where she was loved and nurtured
And developed her special charm.

Unknowingly, 18 years later
Another generation would appear.
Her first born would be a daughter
And in this same farm house she would be loved and reared.

A one-room school met all her needs
At Trenton Elementary.
Her notes were accurate but not too neat,
So her best friend, Dorothy, helped check each entry.

IMMANUEL EVANGELICAL LUTHERAN CHURCH

As a teenager she prepared for the future
Along with other 4-H members.
Her faith kindled through Christian Endeavor
Today still glowing with no smoldering embers.

A deep window sill in the farm kitchen
Was a favorite spot back when
Our mother would sit and recite
Her favorite verse – "The Little Red Hen".

Besides Mom and Dad and two brothers,
Aunt Lola was her favorite aunt.
Carroll, Nolan and Mother made 3,
And soon seeds of a new generation to plant.

It wasn't long before our Mother
Met her very special guy
At a picnic at Trenton Church,
Now, soon, the wedding knot they would tie.

Our mother dated no other
Because Preston was her life.
After two years of dating, they were convinced
That God's plan saw them as man and wife.

June 11, 1932
Was their very important day.
Pastor Shrader pronounced them man and wife
After hearing them promise to love, honor and
obey.

Our mother wore a white dress
With the fashionable uneven hem;
A white straw hat to accent
Making their wedding portrait a lovely gem.

They did not have a honeymoon
Because of the depression years,
But they had fun in the Ford Roadster,
The rumble seat bringing laughter with tears.

Our couple lived with her parents
Until they could afford a place of their own.
Our mother is living there today
On the farm they have always called home.

They set up housekeeping
In the most economical way.
Our mother shopped at public sales
Providing a warmth and coziness that is evident
today.

Sometimes our plans fall through
And we must improvise.
So, when their first born was not a boy,
The nick name of "Juney-Boys" was no surprise.

Six years later they got their boy
And six years after Jim they got Betty;
Then a second family emerged.
With Preston and Vicki, days were active and
ready.

June is her ole standby,
Always there for any call.
Jimmy is her builder
Ready with plans, lumber and saw.

Betty is the kind and gentle one
Who knows that time heals all.
Vicki has received all the honors
And as Mom's nurse, is always "on call".

Our mother loves a baseball game
Especially since Preston is her favorite ballplayer.
Don't be surprised to find her warming up
In case only 8 appear and they need another
player.

SEASONED WITH RHYMES AND A PINCH OF THYME

Our mother has had her chickens
For such a long time
That her children grew up thinking
Any family without chickens was committing a
crime.

Remember the evening Jimmy was missing
And no where to be found?
He was on the roost in the chicken house
Asleep with his family but safe and sound.

Yes, our mother is proud of her children
And there is reason that she should be;
But her in-laws are loved just as much
As if born by her, you see.

She has 6 granddaughters and one grandson
And when each granddaughter started to date,
The boys fell in love with grandma
And the girls thought this was great.

A mother of 6, grandmother of 7
And a great grandmother of 4.
It's not surprising to be told
She forgets which one just came through the door.

Her grandchildren thinks she's neat
Because she becomes one of them, too.
She's just a bigger and wiser kid
Experienced with similar problems as she grew.

She has such a great sense of humor
And loves to tell a good joke.
Sometimes she laughs so hard
Her concentration for the punch line is broke.

Her husband called her "The Madam"
And whatever "The Madam" had to say
Was what settled the questioning issue,
And the children knew to obey.

Our mother and grandmother is very human,
As Vicki and Susan will recall,
When receiving spankings for breaking the towel
rack,
But all ended with a lesson and cookies for all.

She is a very hard worker
And keeping busy is an important need.
With two wood stoves to keep her warm,
Carrying wood is her daily winter deed.

Flowers and plants are a hobby
As you would see on her porch.
Her daughter says you would think it a jungle
If you added a native with a flaming torch.

Plants over your head, at your side,
And also in front of your feet.
Your vision isn't playing tricks
If, in her living room, a tree touching the ceiling
you should meet.

Our mother grows her own vegetables
And loves to freeze and can,
Always keeping little for herself
But shares with her family while lending a helping
hand.

She is a terrific cook
Just ask any family member.
Thanksgiving Day she goes all out
Entertaining 27, as I'm sure they will remember.

Her brother-in-law always said
His favorite was her devils food cake.
A dash of this and a pinch of that
And a delicious goodie ready to bake.

There is something our mother dislikes –
Income tax time just shouldn't be.
I think if we took a vote today,
Many of us would surely agree.

We are fortunate she is here today
Because she is packing to leave.
Our mother is a world traveler
And Europe is on her agenda, I believe.

Friends are so special to her;
Minnie, Gladys and Addie, to name a few.
Whether it be shopping or a public supper,
She has stories to tell you wouldn't think could be
true.

Besides the sport of baseball,
She bowls like you wouldn't believe.
Her Thursday Night League has given her
A nickname only she could achieve.

Now "Lu Lu" had an experience
On the way to bowling one night
When a police car pulled her over
To make sure everything was all right.

Mom, Shelby and Betty
Were riding in the front seat,
While little Amy occupied the back
And thought being chauffeured was pretty neat.

Mr. Officer had another idea
And thought it was rather strange,
With 3 big ones in the front,
Could the little one be estranged?

They laughed all the way to bowling
When they realized how this must have looked.
They were mighty lucky that night
That all 3 didn't get booked.

Fun times like these
Are worth their weight in gold.
Our mother shares her sunny personality
With all those within her fold.

Her fun blends with caring
As she is bus matron for the exceptional school.
Her love and compassion again emerges
As she believes that love is a priceless tool.

Betty makes sure her mom makes the bus
When the weather is not the best.
She listens to the radio announcements
To inform her if it's work or a day of rest.

As her parents cared for her,
In return she did the same.
She learned to drive especially
To be there if they called her name.

Her church and family comes first,
And today she can be proud to say
That all of her children are members of Immanuel
And are here honoring her today.

She was a member of Manchester Ladies
Auxiliary,
And a past Manchester Homemaker,
But her church called for her service
And she chose to commit more time to her Maker.

L.C.W. and The Friendship Bible Class,
Bible Study each Monday night,
And being a church council member
Keeps her calendar booked pretty tight.

Her family has shared happy times,
But there have been heartbreaks, too.
They pull together with strength from their Lord,
And overcome with faith renewed.

Our mother's family considers her their pillar,
And they have received strength from her
example.
Their faith in God has grown
Because her faith, love and patience was so ample.

Her daughter tells us she is hard to surprise
Because she senses their every move.
I hope today is an exception
As her suspicions we now hope to prove.

We wish her the best Mother's Day ever
And God's blessing and years of good health.
Immanuel looks forward to her many years of
service
As her presence is more precious than any amount
of wealth.

With your congregation and family waiting,
And flowers and a day just for you.
Anna Louise Martin Wilhelm,
As Immanuel's Mother of the Year, please come
forth and make your debut.

FROM THE KITCHEN OF: Louise Martin Wilhelm
RECIPE FOR: Hot German Potato Salad
INGREDIENTS: ½ lb. bacon
3½ cups potatoes chopped
1 onion
½ tsp. salt
¼ tsp pepper
1 tbsp. sugar
½ cup vinegar
1 egg beaten

Cook bacon and combine with potatoes and onion. Add rest of ingredients to bacon drippings. Heat and pour bacon drippings over potato mixture and mix.

FROM THE KITCHEN OF: Louise Martin Wilhelm
RECIPE FOR: Dressings for Cole Slaw
Sweet and Sour:
INGREDIENTS: ½ cup of vinegar
1 cup sugar
1½ tsp. celery seed
Stir until dissolved and pour over shredded cabbage.
Creamy Dressing:
INGREDIENTS: ½ cup salad dressing
3 tbsp. sugar
2 tsp. celery seed
Stir until dissolved and pour over shredded cabbage.

Romans 15:2 – "Let each of us please his neighbor for His good to build him up."

IMMANUEL EVANGELICAL LUTHERAN CHURCH

MAY 1985 – IMMANUEL'S MOTHER OF THE YEAR
ELSIE VIRGINIA SHORB

A very popular game today
Is called "Trivial Pursuit",
That digs deep into your memory
For facts that can be important or just cute.

Today I have some trivia
That goes back quite a way
To the very first Mother's Day
Observed in Philadelphia, PA.

May 10, 1908
Miss Anna Jarvis' desire came true.
Through a dream to honor her mother,
A special Mother's Day grew.

May 8, 1914
The first Mother's Day was proclaimed.
President Woodrow Wilson directed
Flags be flown for this special day named.

Many mothers have been honored
Since this date in 1908.
From Immanuel our Mothers of the Year
Have numbered 16 as to date.

And now today we honor
Immanuel's 17th Mother of the Year
To continue the tradition
That has brought surprise and many a loving tear.

SEASONED WITH RHYMES AND A PINCH OF THYME

The trivia you are about to hear
Is trivia of a different kind.
It is so important to her family
Since it's the life of the best mother you could
find.

This time of year
Just suits our mother fine
Because she loves her flowers,
Whether blooming or just a lovely vine.

Violets are her favorite
And this you would surely know.
If you happened to pay her a visit,
Her lovely violets she would proudly show.

Ask her about her favorite pastime
And she will tell you that she's ready
To play endless games of bingo
With Peggy Dienst, her bingo steady.

For almost 79 years
Manchester has been her home.
Having been born in 1906
She had no need to pull up roots and roam.

She lived and worked on her parents' farm
And her job was to watch the cows.
If they got into the cornfields,
She was in trouble and how!

Our mother liked school so much
That she walked a couple miles each day.
Tracey School House and Old Fort,
As well as Manchester School just across the way.

On the site of Manchester Bank
There was once the Katie Utz Hotel
Where our mother cooked and cleaned
And performed her job quite well.

Our mother was the third child
With one brother and four sisters besides.
George and Lillie Markle
Molded and developed close family ties.

Do you remember Whit Sunday celebration
With Memorial Day right behind
When big times were held at Manchester Square –
Picnics, cake walks while wearing the best outfit
you could find?

On one particular Whit Sunday,
As the band played and hats and high-button shoes
paraded,
Our mother's eyes met Charles
And for 54 years their love never faded.

He lived on Water Tank Road
And she lived on Fridinger Mill.
She was picked up in the horse and buggy
With no worries of a gas tank to refill.

Our mother has never learned to drive.
She just feels it's safer, you might say.
You see she once tried to drive a Studebaker
But that big ole shed kept getting in the way.

January 27, 1923
Wedding bells rang that day.
Our mother was married in Black Rock Church
And Reverend M.A.G. Miller blessed them on
their way.

No honeymoon expenses for this couple;
No extras and a lot of fanfare.
They had decided to elope
And save for expenses they would have to bear.

IMMANUEL EVANGELICAL LUTHERAN CHURCH

Before their home on Water Tank Road,
They lived with her in-laws;
A move to Melrose and then Manchester –
So many memories she recalls.

Her husband drove a milk truck
But our mother helped as well.
Bottling milk was her task
So Charles could deliver to neighbors to sell.

He owned and operated public auctions
In Melrose for many a year,
And being a fine craftsman with wood,
His gifts to his children remain priceless and dear.

She worked at Melrose Canning Factory
And Penn Carroll Factory, as well.
At Warehime's Restaurant she baked pies
And her success at this I need not tell.

She worked at Lee's Sewing Factory
And Jacob Brothers, too.
Besides sharing in the income,
She raised and loved her children as they grew.

Many times I have stopped to imagine
While writing this poem for today,
Could I have managed as she did
And accomplished all in such a splendid way?

A very high percentage of mothers
Work outside the home today
And find it difficult to manage
Even with modern conveniences that have come
their way.

Our mother didn't have these luxuries
When raising seven girls and three boys,
But with love for life and faith in God,
She survived while coping with sad times and joys.

Thirteen grandchildren have followed
And now another generation.
She is the great grandmother of fourteen
And delighted in each of God's new creation.

She retired from the sewing factory
At the age of sixty-two
And her children have said "She deserved it"
Needing new interests and hobbies to renew.
Her roots are just as strong in Immanuel
Having been a member since fifteen years of age.
Pastor Leatherman helped plant the seeds of faith
Enriching her family album page by page.

Her family album is priceless
As it proves God's earthly plans.
We must face and grow with hard times
Testing our faith through our praying hands.

She truly is our traditional mother
Loving sewing, mending and baking;
Especially her egg custard pies and jellies
Tested by the Shorb Tasting Experts while in the
making.

You will know her favorite color
If you notice her wearing blue,
And if you hand her a dish of ice cream,
You will have selected another favorite, too.

Not only is she devoted to her family,
But she is also proud of her town.
The Ladies Auxiliary and Rebecca Lodge
Had her support when extra time was found.

When I see her every Sunday
My first impulse has always been
To run up and just squeeze her
For her sweet expression made me wish she was
my kin.

SEASONED WITH RHYMES AND A PINCH OF THYME

I think I should warn her
That she will soon be hugged and squeezed
By her family which surrounds her,
As well as her friends who are so pleased.

We wish her many more generations
And years of bingo, violets and custard pies,
And any other trivia
That brings her fun, pleasure and close family ties.

And now for you a trivia question:
"Who is Immanuel's 17th Mother of the Year?"
I believe we have many correct answers:
Elsie Virginia Markle Shorb, come forth and make your presence here.

FROM THE KITCHEN OF: Elsie Virginia Shorb
RECIPE FOR: Barbecue Sandwiches
INGREDIENTS: 1lb. hamburger
                              1 chopped onion
                              1 tbsp. vinegar
                              1 tbsp. barbecue sauce
                              1 tbsp. Worchester sauce
                              1 tbsp. sugar
                              1 tsp. celery seed
                              ½ cup catsup

Cook onion, vinegar, barbecue sauce, Worchester sauce, sugar, celery seed, catsup together until onions are soft (about 15 minutes). Add hamburger and still till all hamburger is broken up. Cook for about one hour.

FROM THE KITCHEN OF: Elsie Virginia Shorb
RECIPE FOR: Light Fudge Candy
INGREDIENTS: 2 cups sugar
                              ½ cup milk
                              ¼ cup butter
                              1 tsp. vanilla

Cook till mixture forms a soft ball in water. Remove from heat.

Add: 1 tsp. vanilla
                              1 cup of peanut butter
                              1 cup of marshmallow

Beat this and pour into buttered pan.

Sirach 6:15 – "A faithful friend is beyond price. No sum can balance his worth."

IMMANUEL EVANGELICAL LUTHERAN CHURCH

MAY 1986 – IMMANUEL'S MOTHER OF THE YEAR
ANNIE VIOLA MILLER EPPLEY

Have you looked out your window
Or stepped outside and looked around?
You would see the freshness of spring's rebirth
From the blue skies to the blossoming ground.

Spring is the perfect season for Mother's Day
Because it, too, has given birth,
And, it, too, has a new beginning
As one of God's miracles here on earth.

Spring carries its seedlings through winter
Protecting and nourishing each day;
Awaiting for the time new buds and blades appear;
Continuing to love and care in every way.

Spring doesn't have an easy time
Keeping the freshness and color it bears.
April storms and summer's rays
Are tough times seeking tough love and care.

Who, but a mother
Would understand this analogy today.
She knows both pain and joy at birth,
As well as hard times when this joy seems to go
the other way.

Who, but a mother knows
The feeling of life creating within;
The anxiety of nourishing and protecting a child
She will teach to love life and conquer sin.

SEASONED WITH RHYMES AND A PINCH OF THYME

Who, but a mother knows
When they leave the nest and flee
The feeling of abandonment
After decades of nurturing that seedling into a tree.

Who, but a mother knows
When it all begins again,
And she looks into that tiny face
As her grandchild reminds her of way-back-when.

Who, but a mother knows
The feeling of being Immanuel's Mother of the
Year
And the anxiety about to befall her
As her life unfolds for all to hear.

Jefferson, Pennsylvania,
Was her birthplace which she may remember.
She lived there for 10 years
Moving to Maryland to make new friends come
September.

At the age of ten
Lineboro became her home;
Moving on the farm
Provided hard work but lots of acreage to roam.

She was raised in a big family
Being the oldest of eight;
Six brothers and one sister
And to her, a big family was just great.

She and her brothers and sister
Looked forward to special times.
Once a year they went to Carlin's Park
Where fun and food was available for nickels and
dimes.

Crossroad School in Lineboro
Provided our mother with the 3 R's of life
And in 1926, she put them to use
Beginning her career as she became Charlie's
wife.

They were married August 15th
As Reverend Lewis Rehmyer officiated.
As they shared their vows in the parsonage
They were soon to be congratulated.

Soon the sound of little feet
To add to their busy days.
Kenneth was their pride and joy
In many rewarding ways.

Our "Mom" was one of tradition
Mixed with today's "Super Mom" traits.
She worked on the farm and outside the home
While providing all the comforts for her son and
mate.

Dorothy Harper remembers her
As the best neighbor you could ask for.
They loved to exchange their dahlias,
Sharing flowers and vegetables and much more.

Doris Martin shares many memories
Especially times when they just dropped in.
Her delicious sugar cakes and ginger snaps
Would have been eligible for a 1st prize win.

Our mother rose early in the morning
Because milking had to be done;
And then perhaps some sewing for Doris
Or homemade lemonade for her son.

77

IMMANUEL EVANGELICAL LUTHERAN CHURCH

She and Doris picked strawberries
Along the railroad track.
With their gallon buckets and sun bonnets
A lot of laughs and strawberries were brought
back.

They picked blackberries and huckleberries
Early mornings in the woods.
With the morning dew about them,
They didn't get the chiggers as they normally
would.
If you went into our mother's cellar,
The shelves would be lined with jars
Of vegetables, fruits and meats,
As well as her apple butter rating 4 stars.

Their ice house was always filled
And saw dust used to crack the ice.
Friends and family will remember
Always a can of ice cream making visiting very
nice.

I wonder if she remembers
Her black Oldsmobile car.
She had to sit on a cushion
Before she could drive very far.

Her hobbies are making doughnuts,
Quilting and gardening, too.
The delicious oysters served by our Ladies
Auxiliary
Were patted by you-know-who.

The fire company and ladies
Would have been lost without her.
Not only did she organize and pat,
But provided pots and pans in which to stir.

For her ladies who helped in preparing,
She made sure they were fed.
Chicken salad and noodle soup
Were favorites I have heard it said.

Yes, the Ladies Auxiliary to our Manchester Fire
Company
Has been a favorite organization.
Supporting them and their cause
Has made her a lady of dedication.

Senior Citizens is another favorite,
And in 1984 an honor was bestowed her.
She was named The Outstanding Senior Citizen
And an award and celebration did occur.

Even though she pats lots of oysters,
Fried chicken is her preferable dinner.
If she served hot milk sponge cake for dessert,
A dip of ice cream would make it a winner.

The canning and sewing factories
Have been occupations of our mother's.
Because of her loving care and concern,
She has also provided home nursing to others.

Of all the people I have interviewed,
Each told me not to forget
To mention how she always cared
For those in bad health and less fortunate.

She took a Red Cross course,
Which her friends told her she could teach;
Teasing her about the Red Cross card
Was all she wanted in her pocket for a moments
reach.

SEASONED WITH RHYMES AND A PINCH OF THYME

She helped nurse many people
Ranging from young to old.
Friends told her she could doctor
Anything from erysipelas to the common cold.

Our rose will please her today
Because she loves pink and red.
Her garden reflects her love of God's creation
As she nurtures her flower bed.

Harry and Jennie Miller watched her blossom
Since her birth in 1908.
She was to them July 29th –
Their first born in a family of eight.

Our mother is a grandmother
And her five grandchildren are her prize.
As a great grandmother she accounts for four
And her devotion to them is no surprise.

When it's doughnut-making time,
What a treat is in store.
Not only her child and grandchildren,
But her great grandchildren yell for more.

In August of 1976
An open house surprise was held
To celebrate their 50th Anniversary
Allowing them to be catered to for a spell.

Their Golden Anniversary is approaching
And we wish them both the best.
God has given them 60 years of marriage
As they took his hand and together they did the rest.

Immanuel has been her home
From 1927 to this day.
She helped us with many church suppers,
And has served us in many other ways.

Our mother loves all mankind,
And has a love for life.
She has served her church and community,
As well as being a devoted mother and wife.

And now, who but our mother
Would know our Mother of the Year?
Her friends and precious family
Who are seated very near.
Who, but our mother
Knows the joy this moment brings?
Her friends and family sharing this moment
And knowing the happiness she brings in all things.

Who, but our mother
Is feeling the excitement at this time,
And is waiting for her name
To complete this poem of rhyme

Annie Viola Miller Eppley
You are Immanuel's Mother of the Year.
May we honor and congratulate you
As a friend and mother we all hold dear.

We wish you the best Mother's Day ever
And God's blessing and years of good health.
Immanuel looks forward to many more years of service
As your presence is more precious than any amount of wealth.

Please make your presence to us
For a presentation just for you.
As Immanuel's Mother of 1986
Please come forth and make your debut.

FROM THE KITCHEN OF: Annie Viola Miller Eppley
RECIPE FOR: Doughnuts
INGREDIENTS: 2 eggs
                     1 cup shortening
                     1 cup white sugar
                     2 pkg. yeast
                     1 cup mashed potatoes
                     1 tsp. salt
                     3 cups warm water
                     about 5 lb. Pillsbury or Gold Medal flour

Beat eggs and sugar together. Mix yeast in ½ cup warm water and 1 tsp. of white sugar; let set until it starts to foam. Put flour in large bowl (plastic is best). Add about 4 lbs flour and shortening as you mix it with your hands. Let set until it doubles or overnight. Roll out, cut and fry in Crisco or oil in heavy pan until golden brown. Roll in 10x sugar when cold. Makes about 6 dozen.

FROM THE KITCHEN OF: Annie Viola Miller Eppley
RECIPE FOR: Freezer Cole Slaw
INGREDIENTS: 2 cups sugar
                     ½ cup vinegar
                     ½ cup water
                     1 tsp. salt
                     1 gal. cabbage
                     Red and green pepper
                     Onion

Put first 4 ingredients together. Bring to a boil. Cool. Cut cabbage; salt to taste and let sit about 15 minutes. Put in containers. Add peppers and also onion if desired. Add liquid; cover and freeze. Can be kept all winter.

FROM THE KITCHEN OF: Annie Viola Miller Eppley
RECIPE FOR: Strawberry or Peach Glazed Pie
INGREDIENTS: 1 cup water
                     1 cup sugar
                     3 tbsp. cornstarch
                     1 (3oz.) pkg. strawberry Jell-O
                     1 qt. strawberries
                     (You can also use 1 (3oz.) pkg. peach Jell-O
                     And 1 qt. peaches)

Cook water, sugar, cornstarch and Jell-O until clear. Slice fruit. Pour in baked pie shell. Let cool. Top with whipped cream.

Sirach 6:15 – "A faithful friend is beyond price. No sum can balance his worth."

MAY 1987 – IMMANUEL'S MOTHER OF THE YEAR
EDNA REBECCA SCHAEFFER FERRIER

A mother, a child, a flower and a song –
A traditional Mother's Day
Immanuel welcomes each of you
Asking God's blessings in His own special way.

We honor today a special mother –
Immanuel's Mother of the Year;
Bringing memories of yesterday
To a mom whose caring has been so sincere.

There is no doubt mothers are special,
But grandmothers have a special knack
Of adding a special touch with grandchildren
That others seem to lack.

Our mother is a special grandmother
Of three, which she adores;
Waiting for a game of scrabble or cards
When her granddaughter walks through the door.

Grandmothers are the best babysitters –
Ones that money can't buy;
Seldom saying "No, I can't",
But suggesting an overnight stay in reply.

At grandma's rainy days are special
With many adventures in store.
When wandering to the attic,
They find memories waiting to explore.

IMMANUEL EVANGELICAL LUTHERAN CHURCH

The grandchildren spy in the old wooden chest
Wearing many years of dust.
The cobwebs add a touch of class
With the hinges covered with rust.

As the lid is gently lifted,
History begins to unfold
From birth to marriage to newborns,
And locks of hair of angel gold.

Eyes now focus on a treasure –
A picture album of family history;
A one-of-a-kind story book
Featuring romance, adventure and mystery.

As the pages start to turn,
A wedding portrait unfolds;
That of Harry and Mabel Schaeffer –
A premise to our mother's life and all that it holds.

Our couple had five children –
Two boys and three girls they raised.
One of their daughters happens to be
Immanuel's Mother about to be honored and
praised.

A picture on Tracey Mill Road
Of her one-room schoolhouse,
Reminds her of teacher's napping
Behind the pot-belly stove quiet as a mouse.

On her way to school one day,
She and brother found a skunk that was caught.
After visiting and arriving to school,
Little attention was given on what was being
taught.

In winter time walking to school
After a big snow fall on Dug Hill,
She could walk over snow fences
To reach school on Tracey Mill.

A portrait of her family
Reveals she was the oldest of five.
When Mom and Dad stepped out,
Treva Graf babysat this little bee hive.

A page is turned to find a snapshot
Of our Manchester School.
Our mother had transferred from Tracey Mill
To continue learning the Golden Rule.

And now a picture of a handsome beau,
And a portrait of their wedding day.
July 1, 1933, and a new chapter
As Mr. and Mrs. go on their way.

Their marriage took place in Manchester
And Reverend Lewis Rehmyer officiated.
As they shared their vows in the parsonage,
They were soon to be congratulated.

Our mother worked in the sewing factory
And was a waitress, too.
Along with caring for her home,
Grant still came first as her duties grew.

Our family album continues,
And they see a baby boy.
Jim was their first born
Bringing new adventures, love and joy.

Several years later a second son,
And now two boys to keep in line.
Jim wanted a brother,
And Ray was exactly what he had in mind.

Her friend and neighbor, Hilda,
Remembers Halloween
When they took the children trick or treating
Sometimes dressing up themselves or standing
back so as not to be seen.

SEASONED WITH RHYMES AND A PINCH OF THYME

Grant had a huckster route
And his partner by his side.
She continued to be his right hand
As Immanuel's sexton about 1975.

A snapshot of two little guys and a girl –
As cute as they can be.
With children you usually get grandchildren,
And Jim and Ray honored them with three.

Jim and Mark loved to visit
And spend time at Mom and Pop's.
Jenny had their immediate attention,
And to all three, they are just tops.

This family and their friends are my kind of people
They love a spur-of-the-moment party.
Hilda would help her pick strawberries,
And that night, the party had few who were tardy.

The grandchildren turn the page
And find a picture of a birthday cake.
A little lopsided, but I bet delicious
All caused by the way it was baked.

You see, one year Grant forgot her birthday
But called Hilda after dinner requesting a cake for
that night.
Hilda hurried and baked the cake,
But still being warm, the icing and top layer slid
from left to right.

When Grant presented it to his wife
At her party shortly thereafter,
The top layer slid right off
Bringing with it lots of fun and laughter.

Her February 18th birth date
Has been shared by others, as well.
Beatrice and Ralph Hull's anniversary
Automatically rings the dinner bell.

If it wasn't a birthday party,
It was a dinner or trip with the Hulls;
Perhaps to Skyline Drive
Or stopping at hobby shops, flea markets and
malls.

The Hulls wonder if she remembers
The trip in the mountains of Kentucky.
In the pouring rain at 9 p.m.,
If you finally found a motel, you thought you were
lucky.

Their trip to the Carolinas
Reminds the Hulls of that very hot day
When they stopped for a refreshing drink
And was told "not coke, but it's dope down our
way."

Life is slower in the Carolinas
As proven when Grant spied a sign.
It read "Chestnuts – (so much a pound),"
But when ordering, he found it was from
Christmas time.

Enjoying a Sunday drive with you
Were Willie and Hilda Hoff,
Taking back roads and getting lost
With the scenery and ice cream cones, you
couldn't get enough.

Pictures of more good times appear
In the mountains of Snow Shoe, PA.
There's a little country store she loves
With odds and ends where she could spend all day.

Maggie's craft shop in Hanover
Brings her shopping trips to an end.
She's always working on new ideas
To crochet, knit, quilt or just mend.

IMMANUEL EVANGELICAL LUTHERAN CHURCH

A picture of a Christmas tree
And a unique Christmas yard.
Decorations made by our mother –
To duplicate would be extremely hard.

Chain stitch single or double;
Knit one and purl two.
Our mother is always whipping up
A favor or a gift for me or for you.

She crocheted a cup and saucer
For those at her L.C.W. Christmas lunch.
Being chairman of crafts for L.C.W.,
The nursing home has favors either at breakfast,
dinner or brunch.

She's a natural "green thumb"
As her flowers and plants will tell.
Her quilts and 1000 piece puzzles
Give her reason to sit a spell.

Our mother joined Immanuel in 1944,
And has been a pillar to its many needs.
The choir and L.C.W.
Have bloomed where she has sown her seeds.

Remember the annual oyster supper
When a snow fall left us in the lurch.
Our mother had promised to help,
So wearing her boots, she walked to the church.

Sr. Citizens and traveling
Have taken much of their time.
Bus trips, car trips, long trips or short,
If it's with their friends, the experience is sublime.

Our album now shows pictures
Of Nova Scotia and Opryland.
Pages of their favorite trip
Of our western U.S.A. where the scenery was
grand.

The Hulls, Hoffs and Flemings;
The Hoopers and Yinglings, too,
Have shared with them many good times,
Which I'm sure they intend to continue to pursue.

Our mother is a super cook
Especially family roast beef dinners.
If you brought her fudge and homemade ice cream,
You would surely be a winner.

And now a picture of a bride and groom
Cutting a wedding cake.
Their 40th anniversary lawn party at Ray's
For family and friends to partake.

In July of 1983,
Sister Goldie did entertain
With a 50th anniversary lawn party
In the sunshine without a drop of rain.

Fifty-four years they will soon be together
Through sickness and in health.
Their daily prayers and faith in God
Have given them each other being more precious
than wealth.

And now another page,
Another day and time,
Waiting for a special picture
And her life described in rhyme.

We wish you the best Mother's Day ever
With your family, which you adore.
Immanuel looks forward to your service
As God blesses you with good health and much
more.

Our photographer is ready,
The camera has captured the humility in her face.
Edna Rebecca Ferrier, as Immanuel's Mother of
the Year,
Please come forward and take your place.

FROM THE KITCHEN OF: Edna Rebecca Ferrier
RECIPE FOR: Sweet Pickle Chips
INGREDIENTS: 4½ quarts sliced cucumbers
                4 cups vinegar
                3 tbsp. salt
                1 tbsp. mustard seed
                ¼ cup sugar

Bring this syrup to a boil. Add cucumbers and bring to a boil again. Drain off all the syrup and pack in jars.

                Syrup – 2¼ cups vinegar
                4¾ cups sugar
                2¼ tsp. celery seed
                1 tbsp. whole allspice
                Pinch of slum and food coloring

Bring this to a boil and pour over the pickles and seal.

FROM THE KITCHEN OF: Edna Rebecca Ferrier
RECIPE FOR: Mom mom's Fudge
INGREDIENTS: Combine in saucepan:
                4 cups sugar
                4 tbsp. cocoa
                1 cup milk

Boil until it forms a soft ball in cold water. DO NOT STIR. Remove from heat and add: 2 tbsp. butter
                1 jar marshmallow
                1 jar peanut butter

Stir until creamy. Pour into buttered pan. When set, cut into pieces.

FROM THE KITCHEN OF: Edna Rebecca Ferrier
RECIPE FOR: Chocolate Custard Pie
INGREDIENTS: Baked pie shell
                2 eggs (yolks only)
                1 cup water
                2 tbsp. flour
                6 tbsp. sugar
                2 tbsp. chocolate

Boil and fill a single baked pie crust. Beat 2 egg whites and 2 tbsp. sugar until stiff and place on top of pie before serving.

FROM THE KITCHEN OF: Edna Rebecca Ferrier
RECIPE FOR: Country Fried Chicken
INGREDIENTS: 1 (3 to 4 lb.) fryer chicken ¾ cup buttermilk

Coating: 1½ to 2 cups flour
                           1½ tsp. salt
                           ½ tsp. pepper
                           ½ tsp. garlic powder
                           ½ tsp. onion powder
                           1 tsp. paprika
                           ¼ tsp. ground sage
                           ¼ tsp. ground thyme
                           ⅛ tsp. baking powder
                           Cooking oil (for frying)

Wash and pat dry chicken pieces. Place in large flat dish. Pour buttermilk over chicken; cover. Allow to soak 1 hour or refrigerate overnight. Combine coating ingredients in double bag. Shake 1 piece of chicken at a time. Place on wax paper for 10 to 15 minutes to allow coating to dry. Pour oil for frying and heat skillet to 360 degrees. Fry slowly turning often. Drain on paper towels.

Psalm 20:5 "Grant what is in your heart, fulfill your every plan."

MAY 1988 – IMMANUEL'S MOTHER OF THE YEAR
IVA MAE BRILHART YINGLING

How difficult it is each year
For Immanuel's Committee to choose
A special mother to honor
While not wanting any mom to lose.

But only one can be our Mother of the Year
And, again, Immanuel has made a selection.
So, on this festive Mother's Day,
We prepare to show her our sincere affection.

One of her characteristics admired
Is her calm and gentle manner.
If we draped her with a Winner's sash,
"Silence is Golden" would adorn her banner.

Our mother comes from a large family
Having had 4 sisters and 2 brothers.
She remembers lots of good family times
As is happening today with lots of our mothers.

She lives today in Manchester,
But was born almost 72 years ago in Baltimore.
I wonder if she remembers her first day of school
Arriving by horse and buggy as it dropped her off
at the door.

This wasn't always the case.
She usually walked two miles;
We wouldn't have to worry about exercise
If walking was a part of our life styles.

IMMANUEL EVANGELICAL LUTHERAN CHURCH

She was an accomplice playing jokes
When she helped Bud and Mable tease,
Locking Francis in the chicken crate;
Pulling the wagon and hearing her cries and pleas.

Playing in the creek
On a hot and humid summer day;
Mary, Edith and Dick joined the others
While having more good times at play.

Charles and Amanda Reed Brilhart
Were her mom and dad.
They lived on Wilkins Avenue
With 7 children to feed and clad.

But, as the years flew by,
Growing up meant foolishness aside.
As her heart and mind turned to Earl,
On July 18, 1936 she became his bride.

They were married in the parsonage,
And their honeymoon they chose to share
With Catherine and Calvin Fitze
For whom they deeply care.

She worked in the sewing factory
Until the day they were truly blessed
With a little blonde that captured their hearts
Who, I'm sure, by this time you have guessed.

Marian Elaine, born May 24, 1941,
Kept them alert and wide awake.
She became their tree of life
As she and Wayne continue to branch out for their
sake.

She's active in WELCA,
Senior Citizens and Carroll County AARP.
A faithful and dependable member,
Always giving her talents and time for free.

She's a very crafty mother,
And has always loved to sew.
As one of nature's green thumbs,
She can make anything grow.

They both love to travel,
And have done so through Canada and the States.
Florida welcomes them almost every year,
And the Mississippi Queen was exceptionally
great.

They were planning a trip to Texas,
And the departure date was this weekend.
Earl was needed for the Mother-Daughter Banquet,
So his wife agreed rather than to offend.

The trip will still be taken
In perhaps a week or so.
Russell and Mary Brehm will accompany
And, with his cooking behind, Earl will be ready to
go.

Catherine and Calvin Fitze
Have continued to each be a faithful friend.
They make many trips together
As their personalities continued to blend.

In the year 1977,
Another baby was born –
An idea for helping others;
So, she supported Earl as Carroll Lutheran Village
was adorn.

They are members of the Friends of the Village
And some day hope to be their neighbors;
Finally reaping in the rewards
From their hard work, prayers and labors.

Iva Mae Brilhart Yingling,
We honor you today,
As Immanuel's Mother of the Year
And all of our good wishes we convey.

We wish you many more years
Of joy, good friends and good health.
As you share those years with family and friends,
Those assets will outweigh any measure of wealth.

Please come forward now
As we plan to honor you
With lots of applause, flowers and good wishes
From your friends, both old and new.

FROM THE KITCHEN OF: Iva Mae Yingling
RECIPE FOR: Zucchini Casserole
INGREDIENTS:
1½ lb. zucchini, cut ¼ inch
1 lb. ground beef
1 cup onion, chopped
1 cup instant rice
1 tsp. garlic salt
1 tsp. oregano
¼ tsp. basil
¼ tsp. pepper
2 cups small curd cottage cheese
1 can cream of mushroom soup
1 cup grated sharp Cheddar cheese

Cook zucchini in salted water until barely tender. Drain well. Sauté beef with onion until meat is slightly browned. Add rice and seasonings. Place half of zucchini in a 2 ½ quart casserole. Cover with beef mixture and spread the cottage cheese over beef. Add remaining zucchini, then spread soup over all. Sprinkle with grated cheese. Bake uncovered at 350 degrees for 35 to 40 minutes or until bubbly.

FROM THE KITCHEN OF: Iva Mae Yingling
RECIPE FOR: Red Devil's Food Cake
INGREDIENTS:
½ cup butter
2 cups sugar
2 eggs
1 cup sour milk
1 heaping tsp. soda
⅔ cup cocoa
½ cup boiling water
2½ cup flour
1 tsp. vanilla

Cream the butter with the sugar. Add the eggs, sour milk and soda dissolved in hot water. Dissolve the cocoa in boiling water and add to the mixture. Stir in last the flour and vanilla. Bake at 350 degrees for 30 to 35 minutes in 2 (9 inch) cake pans.

Isaiah 60:1 "Rise up in splendor. Your light has come; the glory of the Lord shines upon you."

IMMANUEL EVANGELICAL LUTHERAN CHURCH

MAY 1989 – IMMANUEL'S MOTHER OF THE YEAR
ETHEL BAUST

Today we honor all mothers
In this beautiful season of spring.
What a perfect season to reflect on birth
As we watch trees bud and listen to birds sing.

Spring carries its seedlings through winter
Nourishing and protecting each day
Just as Immanuel's mother has done
By caring for her young in such a loving way.

Our mother's family received in the mail,
About a month before,
A letter saying, "Immanuel is happy to inform ..."
Announcing this honor to be bestowed at her door.

Memories surfaced for information
To share in the poem of her life.
As her family planned for this special day,
They were reacquainted with her as a child, a
mother and wife.

Our mother has always been busy,
And to this day has kept herself even so.
She's always been a good sport
Trying almost anything once before saying, "No".

But, she's never too busy to entertain,
As was proven in 1936,
When her sister and husband visited,
And she had a Sunday dinner to fix.

90

SEASONED WITH RHYMES AND A PINCH OF THYME

She picked up the axe,
Marched out the back door,
Beheaded and cleaned a chicken,
Fried up a dinner and all asked for more.

She has always enjoyed cooking and baking
And this brings more fond memories, as well,
As her children returned from school
Needing a warm welcome and to relax for a spell.

A homemade bread aroma met them,
And with a glass of milk, "Oh, wow"!
You need not ask if the milk was fresh,
Because our mother had just milked the cow.

Loaves of bread have been baked and chickens fried,
And gallons of milk have been poured
Pleasing 6 children, 16 grandchildren and 17 great-grandchildren
This being a small part of why she's so adored.

She was born near Miller, Maryland
On April the 17th
And attended Mt. Zion and Grave Run Schools
Where she grew up in her teens.

I'm sure Carrie and Thomas were her examples
In providing a loving home and care,
And as the third oldest of two sisters and six brothers,
She learned to cook, clean and sew many a tear.

As the oldest daughter, she was responsible
For the youngest child's care and mends,
But this didn't keep her from fun times,
Since her brothers included her with their friends.

Besides having good times with friends,
She enjoyed music of every kind.
When her father bought a new player piano,
This drew many friends home, which she didn't mind.

Her daughters remember their new dresses
Created and sewed by their mother.
She could look at a picture and create it,
An "original" for her girls like no other.

Our mother endured the depression,
And with four children, times were rough,
But she never allowed her problems to win.
Along with her smile, inside she was tough.

Besides providing needs at home,
She has worked away, as well:
Black and Decker, Manchester Pants Factory.
And as the Avon Lady, she might have rang your doorbell.

The Dutch Corner Restaurant
Was her employer for a while,
And The Manchester Drugstore
Offered you her service with a smile.

Our mother keeps a busy schedule
With WELCA and three Senior Citizens groups.
As president of one,
She's kept especially busy leading her troops.

Besides quilting and sewing,
Cooking and crafts,
Square dancing and card playing
Provides her with good times and laughs.

Our mother loves to travel,
And she doesn't need much time to pack.
She flew to Saudi Arabia alone
To visit her son and ride on a camel's back.

Of all the cooking our mother has done,
Chinese is a favorite food.
Most likely she is wearing pink today;
Her favorite color that sets the right mood.

She's such a Good Samaritan,
Always ready and willing to lend
A helping hand to a shut-in
Or a friendly note she might send.

Her family has shared happy times,
But there have been heartbreaks, too.
They pull together with strength from God,
And overcome with faith renewed.

We wish her the best Mother's Day ever
And God's blessings and years of good health.
Immanuel looks forward to her continued service
For her presence is more precious than Immanuel's
wealth.
Her family and friends remember
That she never forgets a birthday
Either by sending a card
Or having a singing telegram delivered their way.

But, today, we reverse the tables
And Immanuel sends the congratulations
To a mother honored not only by family
But one so special to her church congregation.

Happy Mother's Day to you,
Ethel Baust, we honor you.
Would you kindly come before us
As we stand and acknowledge you.

FROM THE KITCHEN OF: Ethel Baust
RECIPE FOR: Pretzel Dessert
INGREDIENTS: 2 cups coarsely crushed pretzels
¾ cup margarine melted in 9 x 13 inch sheet cake pan
in 400 degree oven.

Spread pretzels over melted butter. Mix thoroughly. Press down with bottom of a glass. Bake 8 minutes. Cool.

Filling: Cream together:
1 (8oz.) pkg. cream cheese
1 cup sugar
18 oz. container Cool Whip. Pour over cooled crust.

Topping:
2 cups boiling water
2 pkgs. Strawberry Jell-O
2 (10 oz.) pkgs. Frozen strawberries

Jell 10 minutes. Pour over cheese mixture and refrigerate.

FROM THE KITCHEN OF: Ethel Baust
RECIPE FOR: Sweet Potato Bake
INGREDIENTS: 2 cups sweet potatoes (drained and mashed)
                 4 tbsp. Margarine
                 ¼ cup orange juice
                 ½ tsp. salt
                 1 cup miniature marshmallows

Beat until smooth and pour in greased baking dish. Mix 1 cup miniature marshmallows for the top. Bake at 350 degrees 25 minutes and until marshmallows are slightly brown.

FROM THE KITCHEN OF: Ethel Baust
RECIPE FOR: Baked Custard
INGREDIENTS: Beat: 3 eggs
Add: 1 tsp. vanilla
                 ½ tsp. salt (scant)
                 ½ cup sugar

Heat 2 cups milk until warm. Gradually pour milk in beaten egg mixture. Sprinkle top with cinnamon or nutmeg. Bake at 375 degrees for 35-40 minutes in a pan of water.

FROM THE KITCHEN OF: Ethel Baust
RECIPE FOR: Date and Nut Bread
INGREDIENTS: 3 tbsp. butter
                 2 cups sugar
                 4 cups sifted flour
                 2 eggs
                 1 tsp. salt
                 2 tsp. vanilla
                 1 cup chopped nuts
                 1 package dates cut in pieces.

Pour 2 cups hot water over the dates and add 2 tsp. baking soda. Mix the dates first and let cool while preparing the other ingredients. Mix softened butter, sugar, eggs and vanilla. Add flour, salt and nuts to the date mixture. Bake in ungreased gold lined cans. Fill ½ full (makes 6 cans). Bake 1 hour at 340 degrees. Let cool in cans then run a knife around to loosen. Wrap in foil. Can be frozen. Enjoy!

Jeremiah 17:7 – "Blessed is the man who trusts in the Lord whose hope is the Lord."

CHAPTER II

RHYMES AND THYMES OF RECOGNIZED SERVANTS

OF IMMANUEL LUTHERAN CHURCH

In December of 1969, I completed my term of two years as president of L.C.W. This was my thank you to the wonderful women who helped me through those years:

OUR LUTHERAN CHURCH WOMEN,
IMMANUEL'S RIGHT HAND

Fifteen years ago
Immanuel's ladies reorganized
Unsure of what would develop
But willing to be surprised.

As church secretary at that time,
I felt the apprehension.
The thoughts of would it really work
Caused indecision and tension.

Fifteen years have come and gone
With hours of perspiration.
But, the togetherness felt by one and all
Has been their reward of inspiration.

I was honored to be your president
In 1969 and 1970.
The support that followed me through my term
Was magnificent and heavenly.

SEASONED WITH RHYMES AND A PINCH OF THYME

At this time I would like to share
A poem I wrote in thank you
Including two years of reminiscing
As our L.C.W. grew.

I hope this will bring back memories
To many, many of you
And to our members since that time,
An L.C.W. peek review.

Do you remember two years ago
When we promised to do our best,
To serve our God and serve our church
And to put our problems to rest?

The District Dialogue Team met with us
To help us in any way they could,
But we were very pleased to find
That our ladies were working as they should.

Soon we were asked to plan a party
Since our pastor was leaving in May.
Busy as bees we went to work
For our best wishes we desired to convey.

Graduation soon was upon us
And our graduates we didn't forget,
Nor did we let our Senior Citizens go by
Without showing them they're our assets.

Picnic time was here again
And guess who planned the food,
The games, devotions and serving, too,
Our L.C.W., faithful and true.

Did you hear and have you heard
Immanuel's getting a new pastor.
A shower of food to welcome them
And a housecleaning job to be mastered.

Convention time was now before us
And fifteen of our ladies attended.
Your loyal support and backing
Leaves you all to be commended.

Our fathers and sons we couldn't forget;
Without them where would we be.
So the turkey was roasted and the oysters fried
And with cake came coffee or tea.

I suppose you have heard of Christmas in July,
We were no exception and here's the reason why.
In '68 when we trimmed the tree,
We hung new Chrismons for all to see.

Poinsettias sent out a Christmas glow
As they adorned our altar.
Orders were taken and delivered
So not one thing could falter.

Servicemen were remembered
With boxes of goodies and cheer;
And our shut-ins paid a visit
With a gift and wish for the new year.

The Blue and Gold Banquet
Was our first project in '69.
To Immanuel's sponsored cub pack
We invited them to dine.

Easter time and lilies –
Our altar showed His glory.
The beauty of our lily display
Shared in the Easter story.

Our confirmands and families
Were honored in May.
We were glad to have a little part
In such an important day.

IMMANUEL EVANGELICAL LUTHERAN CHURCH

Summer found our ladies busy
Canning for our Washington residents.
Aromas spread throughout our church -
Incidentally, so was your president.

Fall was approaching
And one thing was sure
Our calendar was filling
And we had only 4 months more.

With a preoccupied president,
A councilmen's dinner and rally,
Perhaps you've been wondering
How we made all things tally.

I'll tell you how
In the sincerest way I know.
You are the ladies of Immanuel
And never fail as pressures grow.

Kathryn, Beatrice, Iva and Peg
And double-duty Ethel, too;
How these leaders led and served
To carry our objectives through.

Ethel and Mary always on the go
Planning, working and taking.
Clothing drives, layettes and much more
While thinking of others in the making.

Five new members for our next term
And eight during our last two years.
That Anne was always on the phone
Telling them why they should be here.

Babies will be babies
And they must be provided for.
So, Betty rocked the cradle
And saw that someone cared for yours.

Communions were always in order
Ribbons in hymnals pressed.
Flowers and cloths in their splendor
Because Edna always did her best.

"Topic, topic, who has the topic?"
Joyce inquired with concern.
Her main goal in education
Was for one and all to learn.

Treva, our chief cook and bottle washer,
Was always in that kitchen
Either getting into trouble
Or a delicious meal she was fetchin'.

News and pictures, clippings, too,
Reports and articles read.
Bessie was always on the job
As Historian she surely led.

Doris' talent with figures
Was for our benefit I'm sure,
Being our efficient treasurer
Kept us from becoming poor.

Respectfully submitted
Our secretary, Sharon,
Efficient with notes and typing
And still her eye on Darin.

My helping hand and stand-in
Was your vice president and mine.
Shirley, always willing and able;
A more conscientious person you just won't find.

Now officers are needed
And, of course, our leaders, too,
But they couldn't have done all the work
And carried all things through.

All of you ladies have been my right arm
Without you we wouldn't be.
You will never know what your devotion has
meant
To a person as grateful as me.

Tonight we move ahead once more
Starting our 7th year.
The promises made before God tonight
Will make our objectives quite clear.

Tonight is just another thank you
For inviting me to share
Two years of special memories,
As well as two years of your concern and care.

The hand of God had guided you
Each step of your active way
And my wishes and prayers are his continuance
As you serve Him every day.

A thank you seems so little to give
But I guess it will have to do,
So to each and everyone tonight,
I do sincerely thank you.

December, 1969

FROM THE KITCHEN OF: Bonnie R. Hull
RECIPE FOR: Chocolate Chip Cookies
INGREDIENTS: Cream together:
1 cup butter-flavored shortening
¾ sugar
¾ packed brown sugar
2 eggs
1 tsp. vanilla

Add:
2¼ cup flour
1 tsp. baking soda
½ tsp. salt

Fold in:
1½ cup semi-sweet chocolate morsels
½ cup finely chopped walnuts (optional)

Bake on ungreased cookie sheets at 350 degrees for 15 minutes. Cool on paper towel. Enjoy warm with glass of milk or cup of tea or coffee!

IMMANUEL EVANGELICAL LUTHERAN CHURCH

FROM THE KITCHEN OF: Bonnie R. Hull
RECIPE FOR: Turkey Ovenburgers
INGREDIENTS: 1½ lb. lean ground turkey
                    2 tbsp. chopped onion
                    2 tbsp. ketchup or mustard
                    1 tsp. salt
                    Dash of pepper
                    ½ tsp. Worcestershire sauce
                    ½ cup bread crumbs (1 slice bread)
                    1 egg

Preheat oven to 350 degrees. Mix above ingredients and form into six patties. Place in a shallow oven baking dish and bake 20 to 25 minutes. A barbecue sauce may be spread on the top before baking or after baking when served if desired.

Psalm 37:7 – "Be still before the Lord and wait patiently for him."

98

SEASONED WITH RHYMES AND A PINCH OF THYME

On Saturday, March 7, 1970, Mrs. Charles Miller was honored for forty years of service to Immanuel Lutheran Church as Financial Secretary. I was asked to present her with the following poem.

This evening we pay an honor
To a lady we all know and love;
A lady of true devotion
To her church and to her God above.

She's in the spotlight this evening
With an orchid corsage to wear.
Her beautiful smile is present
As our memories we would like to share.

Mrs. Mandilla Miller
Is our honored lady's name.
Or, do you know her as "Dillie"?
If so, the name is the same.

Let's go back a little ways
Say eighty years ago
When on that very first day of March
A cradle rocked to and fro.

Mandilla Burkheimer had just been born
And oh what a happy day.
I bet the work was left undone
On that Lineboro farm that day.

Her confirmation day
Was held in Lazarus Church.
For a more sincere church member
You would have had to really search.

IMMANUEL EVANGELICAL LUTHERAN CHURCH

December 6, 1911 and
Lazarus Parsonage was the place
When Burkheimer changed to Miller
And a brand new life they faced.

Dr. Leander Zimmerman
Was asked to tie the knot.
Now Mr. and Mrs. Charles Miller
Chose Baltimore as their first home spot.

As we all know by now
Time constantly advances
And in April of 1913,
A baby arrived named Frances.

Their daughter was always a joy
And proved so in later years,
For she became a teacher
And an asset in her career.

Millers Station and Manchester
Were two more places called home.
A transfer from Lazarus to Immanuel
And from here they did not roam.

Our Cradle Roll was organized
When Pastor Rehmeyer served.
As superintendent and teacher,
Mrs. Miller was reserved.

Immanuel's Financial Secretary
Was Mr. Miller's position,
And upon his death in 1930,
His wife took on this mission.

A brand new home
Was moved to in 1951.
Now Westminster is the address
And a new location in life begun.

Figures, envelopes and meetings
Took a large part of forty years.
There were very few meetings and Sundays
When Mrs. Miller didn't appear.

From 1926 to 1955
Booklets of statements were sent.
Columns and columns of figures were totaled
So we know where her time was spent.

Pastors Rehmeyer, Shanebrook, Miller and
Kretschmer
Were four pastors which she served.
And working with nine different treasurers
Proves that her patience and efficiency is well
preserved.

Seventy-five different men and women
Have worked on the council with her.
At the slightest question of money,
They sought Mrs. Miller to confer.

We don't know how she did it
But everyone's envelope number she knew,
And she never just double checked her work
But re-checked it through and through.

After every service
Any day of the week,
Mrs. Miller would be supervising
For offerings and envelopes she did seek.

Stuffing, sealing and tying
Statements, Visitors and such.
Just a few more tasks included
To give a job the finishing touch.

Remember the year the books were closed
With a balance of $6.06?
However the accounts never closed in the red
And we never fell over the fence.

She was an Aid Society officer
And a faithful member, too.
And in the Missionary Society,
Her services grew and grew.

She's always been a busy bee
And still continues so.
She's a member of L.C.W.
And as hostess she naturally glows.

Some day on Pennsylvania Avenue
As you are driving by,
If you slow down just a trifle
You'll smell her favorite coconut cream pie.

But, whatever you do don't give her a call
If your snake's caught up in her tree,
Because two of the biggest fears she has
Are height and snakes, you see.

Yes, Mrs. Miller,
We know all about you,
Even the obvious fact
That your favorite color is blue.

But blue is the wrong word
When describing your mood and manner;
For your beaming personality
Flows to all like a flying banner.

Forty years is a long time
And you truly deserve a rest.
Immanuel's 800 members
Thank you for doing your very best.

We also thank God for sharing you
With us through many a year.
May He watch over and give happiness and health
To a lady we all hold dear.

March 7, 1970

FROM THE KITCHEN OF: Mandilla "Dillie" Miller
RECIPE FOR: Coconut Cream Pie
INGREDIENTS: 1 baked pie shell
                 1½ cup milk
                 ½ cup sugar
                 1 egg beaten
                 ½ cup milk
                 2 heaping tbsp. cornstarch
                 Pinch of salt
                 ½ tsp. vanilla

Put the sugar in a saucepan. Add the 1 ½ cup milk; heat until it just comes to a boil. Mix the beaten egg with ½ cup milk and the cornstarch. Add to the hot milk to thicken. Add coconut. Cool and pour into baked pie shell. If you like, you can top with meringue made from egg whites and sugar and cream of tartar. Beat until stiff, put on top of pie and brown in 350 degree oven for 12 to 15 minutes (optional).

Psalm 75:2 – "We thank you, God, we give thanks; we call upon your name, declare your wonderful deeds."

101

HAPPY 25TH ANNIVERSARY
REVEREND AND MRS. ELLIS KRETSCHMER

The month was May
And the year was '68
When two strangers came to town
For a very important date.

Manchester, Maryland?
Do you think it's on the map?
I feel we'll be driving for hours.
Says he, "Kretschmer, ole Boy, it's time for a nap".

But, alas, their destination
And the Pulpit Committee awaited
To greet Pastor and Mrs. Kretschmer
For possibly a new pastor was slated.

Meetings, letters and decisions
And a trial sermon in July.
The "Four D's of Discipline" given
And Immanuel's consent wasn't denied.

What a good feeling to know
That we had a pastor again.
A fine leader and organizer
And a great teacher to comprehend.

Mrs. Kretschmer spent her time
Traveling to and fro;
Visiting with the Yinglings
And then back to Philly she would go.

Helping to pack boxes of books
To be moved on moving day,
And then unpacking those boxes of books
Was enough to cause dismay.

A pantry shower surprise
Greeted the Kretschmers on their return
And now a new life was beginning
As the Kretschmers soon were to learn.

SEASONED WITH RHYMES AND A PINCH OF THYME

Installation Sunday
Was a very special day,
And friends from Philadelphia
Shared in their own special way.

Now with all the unpacking
Of bric-a-brac and books,
Double duty came to Mrs. K.
Being organizer, teacher and cook.

Mrs. Kretschmer teaches first grade
At our Manchester School.
She has taught for twenty-five years
How to live by the Golden Rule.

She likes to travel with hubby
Sharing his interest in music, too.
Along with loving to travel,
Cruises are a special treat, too.

Other than Pastor Kretschmer,
There's someone else in her life.
He's white, fluffy and angora –
The perfect pet for a busy wife.

His name is Whitey Kretschmer
And his age is thirteen years.
He loves hog kidneys for dinner
But to be brushed he definitely fears.

One of the first shocks
That Immanuel's members received
Was a large church attendance
On Thanksgiving Eve.

Remember the Pastor's first Christmas here
And our beautiful poinsettia display?
A spectacular sight for all to behold
As we approached Christmas Day.

On Christmas Day at the Kretschmers,
A delicious dinner you will find
Of duck or goose and the trimmings
And everyone anxious to dine.

Because pastors warm leftovers
In aluminum pie pans with holes,
Frocks has been rated o.k.
With the Kretschmers we are told.

If we have failed to welcome guests
They won't feel left out for long.
Just give them time to meet our Pastor
And his handshake will patch up our wrongs.

I don't know what we put in coffee
That make our pastors frown,
Bur another tea drinker
Has come to our small town.

In lent for 40 days and nights
Our Pastor gives up sweets.
But you better bet he has on hand
English muffins ready to eat.

We know they are quite happy
With their home up on the hill,
And Mrs. Kretschmer has found time
To add the beauty of flowers where she will.

"We're friends even though
We don't always agree,"
Is a favorite statement
Of our Pastor when he must disagree.

Philadelphia is still a highlight
In the life of Pastor K.
He travels to play his violin
In the Little Symphony four hours away.

IMMANUEL EVANGELICAL LUTHERAN CHURCH

If you enjoyed "The Little Foxes"
Then you have a treat in store.
We were told the "Yellow Sweater" and
"Umbrella"
Will keep you in stitches even more.

There are some Philadelphians
Who have asked us to let them know
The Sunday the donkey comes down the aisle
With our Pastor bouncing to and fro.

His sermons are so powerful
And "hits home" with everyone,
Leaving afterthoughts for one and all
And a new way of life begun.

Westminster District Cabinet and
American Missions, too,
Go along with extra duties
That our Pastor must find time to do.

Our Pastor has a great desire
To drive a fire truck someday.
We understand he would do quite well
Since he drives his car the same way.

However, our Pastor has a connection
With our Fire Company here.
He is the Volunteer Fire Chaplain
And is on call anytime of the year.

June 17, 1945
Will now be remembered by us,
So wishes of congratulations
Each year will be a must.

However, we hope you will forgive us
For going behind your backs,
But surprises must be hush, hush
To keep honored guests off the track.

There is one little thing
That didn't work out quite right.
You were taken out to dinner
But not to Allenberry tonight.

I'm sure you will overlook this
And realize our good intentions,
But you know we're really very good
At other sneaky inventions.

Twenty-five years of marriage
Blessed with happiness and good health,
New faces, places and experiences
Included in your mountain of wealth.

Pastor and Mrs. Kretschmer,
Our wish for you tonight
Includes more of the past twenty-five years
And good times to be your delight.

FROM THE KITCHEN OF: Bonnie R. Hull in honor and memory of Pastor and Mrs. Kretschmer. This recipe was given to me by Miss Adda Trump, a very special member of Immanuel. RECIPE FOR: Scripture Cake INGREDIENTS: ½ cup Judges 5:25 (butter), 1 cup Jeremiah 6:20 (sugar), 3 Isaiah 10:14 (eggs), 3 tbsp. I Samuel 14:25 (honey), ½ tsp. Leviticus 2:13 (salt), 2 cups I Kings 4:22 flour, 2 tsp. Amos 4:5 (baking powder), 2 tsp. II Chronicles 9:9 (spice – 1 tsp. each of cinnamon and nutmeg), ½ cup Judges 4:19 (milk), 1 cup Nahum 3:12 chopped figs, 1 cup Numbers 17:8 (sliced almonds), 1 cup I Samuel 30:12 (raisins), Cream butter and sugar, add honey and beaten yolks. Add remaining dry ingredients alternately with milk. Stir in fruit and nuts. Fold in beaten egg whites last. Bake at 325 degrees for 45 minutes in a 9 x 13 pan. Serve with whipped cream topping.

TO PASTOR KRETSCHMER:
OUR CONFIRMATION DAY – MAY 30, 1971

Our Confirmation Day
Is approaching very fast.
Since we began our studies,
Two years have quickly passed.

It took a lot of studying
And concentrating, too;
An extra little push
To tackle something new.

And now here we are
Only one day away
From May 30, 1971,
Our Confirmation Day.

We have had a teacher
Whose patience was so great
In getting us through the chapters
And keeping us up to date.

You added moments of humor
Like a jiggle now and then.
This we all enjoyed
Because we never knew just when.

Many duties were a chore
When they were first assigned,
But sermon notes helped to comprehend
As well as memorizing lines.

Pastor Ellis Kretschmer
You we will never forget.
The big step we take tomorrow
Is because of your Christian Assets.

You have given us much
That will guide us through the years,
And we will always be grateful
For the teachings we absorbed here.

Our Class of 1971	May God bless you
Thanks you sixteen times	Each and every day
Because sixteen of us	With all His bountiful blessings
Think you are mighty fine.	Which you deserve in every way.

FROM THE KITCHEN OF: In Honor of the Confirmation Class of 1971

RECIPE FOR: Easter Jelly Beans
Red is for the Blood He gave,
Green is for the grass He made.
Yellow for His sun so bright,
Orange is for the edge of night.
Black is for the sins we made,
White for the grace He gave;
Purple for His hours of sorrow,
Pink is for our new tomorrow.
A bag of jelly beans
Colorful and sweet;
Is a prayer! Is a promise!
Is a special treat!
(Taken from Amish Home Cooking with Elsa)

Psalm 85:8 "Show us Lord your love; grant us your salvation."

"OUR MUSIC MAN, JESSE L. BETLYON"

The walls of Immanuel
Began to swell
When our men joined together
With a story to tell.

They had talent
And they wanted it shown,
Just another step
Showing how Immanuel had grown.

It was the spring of '52
When they decided to sing,
But the do, re and mi
Just had an awful ring.

Mr. Jesse Betlyon
Was asked to lend a hand
And before you knew what happened,
They were singing rather grand.

This "music man" who came our way
Was rather quite contagious.
The high school, junior and adult choirs
Proved he was quite courageous.

One, two, three and four –
That's what our leader said.
He snapped his fingers right in time
As his choirs were joyously led.

Junior Choir began at 7:00
Followed by the teens.
Sixty minutes later,
The adult choir was seen.

After arriving for junior choir
At 7:00 on the dot,
He would remember at the piano
His glasses he forgot.

At 7:30 p.m.
Patrolman he became
As the high school choir he hunted
As if time allowed for playing games.

He would find them on the front steps
Or wandering down the hall,
And shortly after beginning
Came Garth from playing football.

IMMANUEL EVANGELICAL LUTHERAN CHURCH

Did you ever save that article
That you were to bring for Scott?
We don't know much about it
But we bet that you forgot.

Remember how the choir broke up
With "little fishies, too"?
That anthem perhaps was never sung
If Beverly and Karen talked to you.

Was there ever any question
What to sing at Christmas time?
How about "Birthday of a King"
Or "O Holy Night," the choir would chime.

The choir members liked to tease
As you wandered through the pews –
Did the anthem sound that terrible
Or perhaps nervous anxieties grew?

Most adult choir members
Arrived at half past 8:00
Except for Marshall Dillon fans
Or if Bob's zipper happened to break.

First a drink of water –
Mr. B. was all sung out –
Then the cough drops and Vick's inhaler
And then he was ready to shout.

"Cathy, Cathy, Cathy,
You're playing it all wrong!
And really, Bernard,
You held that note too long!"

"You guys on that back row
You're singing the wrong tune,
And, girls, you must watch me
So you don't sing in too soon."

"Please watch me people
On that do, re, mi, fa, so.
I'm not much to look at
But I'm heaven to know."

How would so few members
Prepare the anthem planned?
Dig out the old green book –
It falls open without any hands.

Busy, busy, busy
No time to prepare for Sunday.
So, "Master We Come To Thee"
Was practiced on Monday.

Cantatas added oh so much
Especially with added help,
And Mr. Betlyon's directing
Was most definitely felt.

Choir parties followed cantatas,
Evaluation, fun and food.
Remembering hymn sings in little churches
Put all in a giggly mood.

Our Choir Master
Had to be a clown
To put up with the men's back row
Which kept him going round and round.

Remember the choir lady recessing
Who caught her heel in a grill
The grill she took right with her
Leaving the hole for the tenor to fill?

Mr. Betlyon was always at rehearsals
Come fog, snow or rain.
Then the lonely drive to Hanover
And one night a State Trooper he gained.

Mr. Betlyon was always summoned
When our pianos were not in tune,
And, then to test his work that day,
He played "Shine on Harvest Moon."

"How Great Thou Art" and songs from "Elijah"
Are some favorites of Mr. B's.
Music of Wright, Goodman and Miller
Makes him relax with ease.

Your life has been a melody of songs
At home, at work and at church.
To the folks at Homewood Home,
You've brought the happiness for which they
search.

Now that there is free time,
We understand there are plans
To form a corporation
With father and sons of the Betlyon clan.

We see there are no retiring plans
In any shape or form
For a man who has always been on the go
From the day that he was born.

What can we say to a man like you
Who has given us so much
Except a big sincere thank you
And our promise to keep in touch.

You are such a special person
To all of us here tonight
And we wish you the best of everything
And hope future plans turn out just right.

Your prayer that you have prayed with us
We always will remember
Because it was a sincere part of you
Each Monday from January through December.

"Our Gracious Heavenly Father
As we enter Thy house again
We thank Thee for all blessings
Which Thou has seen fit to send."

"Help us that we do our best
Each and every day,"
And may your blessings always shine
On "Our Music Man", we pray.

FROM THE KITCHEN OF: Bonnie R. Hull In Memory of Jesse Betlyon by the choirs.
    RECIPE FOR: Oysters on the Half Note
    INGREDIENTS: 2 dozen fresh oysters on half shell
                      4 oz. butter
                      1 scallion, minced
                      Several slices of turkey bacon minced
                      2 tsp. prepared horseradish
                      $\frac{1}{8}$ tsp. Worcestershire sauce
                      $\frac{1}{8}$ tsp. basil, crushed
                      Salt and pepper
                      Rock salt
                      1 lemon sliced
                      Fresh parsley

Wash and shuck the oysters. Leave oysters in curved half shell. Place butter in a mixing bowl and cream at room temperature. Blend in scallion, bacon, horseradish, Worcestershire sauce and basil. Season lightly with salt and pepper. Place a layer of rock salt in shallow baking pan that is large enough to hold oysters in one layer. Heat rock salt in 400 degree oven for 10 minutes. Place a teaspoonful of the butter mixture on each oyster . When salt and pan are hot, arrange oysters carefully on bed of salt. Bake 6 minutes or until the bacon sizzles. Do not overcook. Serve piping hot as appetizer or entree with a garnish of lemon and parsley.

FROM THE KITCHEN OF: Bonnie Hull in memory of Jesse Betlyon by the choirs.
RECIPE FOR: Chicken Piccata
INGREDIENTS: 4 whole skinless and boneless chicken breasts
½ cup flour
1½ tsp. salt
¼ tsp. freshly ground pepper
¼ cup clarified butter
1 tbsp. olive oil
2-4 tbsp. dry white wine
3 tbsp. lemon juice
Lemon slices
¼ cup fresh chopped parsley

Cut breasts in half and pound chicken breasts thin between two sheets of wax paper. Combine flour, salt , pepper, paprika. Coat chicken breasts with mixture. In large skillet, heat butter and oil and sauté breasts until golden (3-4 minutes per side). Place on platter and keep warm. Stir wine into skillet; scrape bottom to loosen all drippings; add lemon juice; blend well. Return chicken to pan and continue to cook until sauce thickens. Add lemon and parsley and serve immediately.

Psalm 147:7 "Sing to the Lord with thanksgiving; with the lyre celebrate our God."

In December of 1971, Peggy Cullison became our L.C.W. President for a two-year term and I was asked to write a thank-you poem at the end of her term.

THANK YOU, PEGGY

It happened on December 19th
And the year was 1971
When Peggy became our president
And now two years later, her job is done.

Peggy, you've done a great job
And "thank you" isn't enough to say,
So we would like to look back on your term
And reminisce a little, if we may.

Your term had a new beginning
With new groups forming in September.
Past years we weren't that prepared
Because we didn't form until December.

A new committee came about
With revival of dinners and receptions.
Caring for and ordering of tablecloths
Put Hilda in charge of inspection.

Now the Pastor is sure to have
Some helpers at the Home.
Peggy assigned each group their turns
Now singing through the halls we roam.

During her administration
Our church parlor took on a new face.
Chandelier, drapes and carpet
Made our parlor a very lovely place.

111

Kathryn Orso had the spotlight
At one of our general meetings.
With other churches attending,
We gave her a room full of greetings.

Need to check on your husband?
Well, ladies, we can do it now.
We have a telephone available
And in emergencies proves to be a real pal.

We all became parents again
When we decided to sponsor Sawait.
Through the Christian Children's Fund,
We made it possible for him to be taught.

Sponsoring Sawait proved to be fun
Especially in September of this year.
We held a hat sale to provide for him
And displayed original creations, prizes and
cheers.

Very few things were forgotten
As Peggy's calendar was planned,
But her mother remembered in '72
Forgotten palms to be striped by hand.

With a telephone and willing workers
Peggy knew she need not worry.
The palms were striped and ready
Without too much worry and hurry.

1972 was convention year
At Gettysburg, P.A.
Peggy was our delegate
And her hubby accompanied her one day.

When the month of August passes,
Busy times begin again
And in 1972,
An extra project to contend.

A Uganda family needing a home and friends
Was heading Immanuel's way.
Someone had to get the ball rolling
And our busy president volunteered without delay.

"Would you please"
And "Would you have time?"
Before you knew what happened
A home was furnished and shiny as a dime.

The Turks were our "Operation Friendship"
And what a great experience for all.
To be able and want to give of ourselves
Proved us true Christians to His call.

"Hark the Herald Angels Sing"
And by bus we did just this
Singing carols throughout Manchester
Was something we had missed.

We went home from our general meeting
In December of '72
With a glorious Christmas feeling
Which the candlelight service renewed.

We gave God our personal commitments
This Christmas of '72,
And from our L.C.W.,
We committed ourselves, too.

One commitment included
Traveling to Washington, D. C.
So a program was presented to the Home
And the response lifted our hearts with glee.

Key '73
Helped us to produce
A six-week Lenten Bible Study
Which six L.C.W. leaders introduced.

Sharing proved very important
With our neighbors at St. Mark's.
We shared a progressive dinner and topic
And received very favorable remarks.

Our president is not only a great leader,
But a fine seamstress she proves to be
And with L.C.W. demands,
Was found working late to please customers, you
see.

Her church work comes first
As she has often said,
And her many hours of devotion
Weren't all obligations but pleasures instead.

She is very active on the choir
And teaches Sunday School.
She serves on church committees
And "lend a helping hand" seems to be her rule.

When vacation time arrived,
She deserved a well earned rest,
And you found her with her family
Camping and scheduling L.C.W., she would
confess.

An old tradition came back to Immanuel,
Thank-offering boxes, that is,
And with this we conducted the service
And Peggy's ladies proved to be a wiz.

One day our pretty white tablecloths
Began to complain.
Their tea stains were showing
And they cried, "Oh, what a shame."

So with very special care,
They are used only for special occasions,
And new green lace paper ones
Now take the tea stain abrasions.

Who are we?
And what do we do?
Now an introductory booklet
Explains this to members who are new.

These are just the main things
That Peggy's administration introduced,
But there were so many other things
That she too had to produce.

Plans for Blue and Gold,
Graduates and confirmands,
Mother-Daughter banquets,
And District Rally demands.

L. C. M. district meetings,
Picnic plans to make,
Senior Citizens to honor,
What group should cook and bake?

Father and Sons were hungry,
A workday to sew and create,
Stamps, stockings and coupons,
Our projects completed were great.

Projects were a big thing
Especially with Christian Service Committee,
Bed jackets, dresses and bandages
Were just a few sent to another city.

A Chrismon tree to be trimmed,
Executive meetings to plan,
Stocking money and a new budget –
Her thoughts looked for place to land.

Peggy has truly been dedicated
And this we all agree.
I would like to share a perfect example
Which I witnessed in '73.

113

On May 11, 1973
Peggy's group had a date
To set up tables for Mothers and Daughters
And to place favors at each ones plate.

Why was I surprised
When it was her duty any way?
Because I thought she would want to b home
Enjoying and celebrating her birthday.

As I walked into the room
I was so surprised to see
Peggy setting tables
And working as hard as could be.

Yes, dedicated Peggy is
And her achievements surely show this.
Tonight she doesn't step down
Because District work she couldn't resist.

Peggy, we wish you the greatest achievement
As you take on greater demands.
And now will you accept our thanks
With an applause from many grateful hands.

FROM THE KITCHEN OF: Peggy Cullison
RECIPE FOR: Homemade Root Beer
INGREDIENTS: ½ pkg. dry yeast
1 cup lukewarm water
3 cups sugar
¾ cup Sweet 'n Low
Warm water to make 4 ¾ gallons
1 bottle root beer extract (Hires or McCormick)

Dissolve yeast in measuring cup of warm water. Place in large 5 gallon container. Add sugar, Sweet 'n Low, root beer extract and warm water to make 4 ¾ gallons. Stir. Place in clean gallon plastic milk jugs to within 2 inches of top. Cap tightly. Set in warm place 3 to 5 days. Bubbles will form inside jugs and they may swell. Taste; when desired strength is obtained, refrigerate. The sugar is necessary to make the yeast work. Keeps 3 to 4 weeks. Makes 5 gallons.

FROM THE KITCHEN OF: Peggy Cullison
RECIPE FOR: Crab cakes
INGREDIENTS: ½ lb. crabmeat or flaked fish
1 ½ tbsp. mayonnaise
3-4 crumbled crackers
½ tsp. mustard
2 tbsp. chopped onion
1 beaten egg
Salt, pepper, Worcestershire Sauce, and Old Bay Seafood Seasoning to taste. Pat into cakes and fry or broil until brown.

Colossians 3:14 "Clothe yourselves with love which binds everything together in perfect harmony."

L.C.W. INSTALLATION SERVICE

At our general meeting on December 15, 1975, the L.C.W. had their annual installation service of new officers and leaders. I wrote the following verses to the tune of "Let There Be Peace on Earth".

Praising God in candlelight
We prepare for another year
Serving Him through all our deeds
In Church and Community.

With God as our Father
Sisters all are we,
Sharing, planning and serving
In perfect harmony.

Tonight we promise Thee
Our devotion and loyalty.
With every step we take
We pray with sincerity.

To take each moment and
Live each moment for
Lutheran Church Women are we.

God bless us all tonight
As we pledge our hearts to Thee.

RECIPES FROM SOME OF OUR L.C.W. MEMBERS AT THAT TIME

FROM THE KITCHEN OF: Jeanne Beaver
RECIPE FOR: Lemon Bars
INGREDIENTS: 1 cup margarine
                ¼ tsp. salt
                2 cups flour
                ½ cup 10x sugar

Mix the above and use pastry cutter. Pat into 9 x 12 pan. Bake 350 degrees for 20 minutes.

                4 eggs
                2 cups sugar
                4 tbsp. flour
                10 tsp. lemon juice

Beat the above well. Pour over baked cookie crust. Bake at 350 degrees for 25 minutes. Sprinkle with 10x sugar if desired. Cut in bars.

FROM THE KITCHEN OF: Anna Miller
RECIPE FOR: Yogurt Dip
INGREDIENTS: 1 cup plain, low-fat yogurt
                1 tbsp. frozen orange concentrate
                1 tsp. lemon juice
                2 pk. Artificial sweetener

Mix. Serve with fruit in pick-up sizes. Also good with Jell-O. This recipe is especially good for diabetics.

FROM THE KITCHEN OF: Esther Singer
RECIPE FOR: Dottie's Chicken
INGREDIENTS: 4 or more cups cooked, cubed chicken
                1 can cream of chicken soup
                1 cup milk
                1 can cream of mushroom soup

Herb Dressing Mix: 1 pkg. Pepperidge Farm Stuffing mix
                1 cup boiling water
                ¼ lb. margarine

Layer cubed chicken in 2 quart casserole. Mix 1 cup milk with soups. Pour over chicken. Top with herb season dressing. Crumble over chicken and bake 1 hour at 350 degrees uncovered. Serves 6.

FROM THE KITCHEN OF: Beatrice Hull
RECIPE FOR: Pineapple Rice
INGREDIENTS: 1 cup whole grain rice
                 1 cup water
                 ½ gallon whole or 2% milk
                 1¾ cups sugar
                 1 pinch of salt
                 ½ stick of margarine or butter
                 1 tsp. vanilla

Boil rice and water until moisture almost gone but still a little runny. Add milk, sugar, salt and margarine and cook very slow for 2 hours at least stirring occasionally. When mixture begins to thicken but not thick, remove from heat, cool, add vanilla and cover with waxed paper and refrigerate.

                 1 can crushed pineapple
                 4 egg whites
                 1 tsp. cream of tartar

Drain a can of crushed pineapple. Beat 4 egg whites with ½ cup sugar and 1 tsp. cream of tartar until stiff. Gently fold into rice pudding and serve.

FROM THE KITCHEN OF: Hilda Hoff
RECIPE FOR: Apple Butter
INGREDIENTS: 7 lb. apples
                 3 cups sugar
                 1 cup vinegar or cider
                 2 tbsp. cinnamon
                 16 cups applesauce

Cook apples until soft; press through sieve or use fork to make smooth. Add remaining ingredients. Put in crock-pot or oven (bake 3 ½ hours at 350 degrees; stir occasionally.)

In crock-pot, cook until thick, 5 to 6 hours. Put in jars and seal. Makes 5 quarts. What a delightful aroma your house will have especially on a nice, cool fall day.

FROM THE KITCHEN OF: Mary Weaver
RECIPE FOR: Cheese Ball
INGREDIENTS:　　16 oz. soft Cheddar cheese
　　　　　　　　16 oz. American cheese, softened
　　　　　　　　6 oz. soft cream cheese
　　　　　　　　2 tbsp. Worcestershire sauce
　　　　　　　　1 tsp. Tabasco sauce
　　　　　　　　1 tsp. garlic juice

Grate cheese and blend the above ingredients into 1 large or 2 medium balls. Serve with crackers or vegetables.

FROM THE KITCHEN OF: Martha Foard
RECIPE FOR: Sweet Potato Casserole
INGREDIENTS:　　3 cups cooked, mashed sweet potatoes
　　　　　　　　1 cup sugar
　　　　　　　　1 tsp. vanilla
　　　　　　　　½ cup melted butter
　　　　　　　　2 eggs beaten
　　　　　　　　⅓ cup milk

Mix first 6 ingredients together and fold into a greased 2 quart casserole. Mix topping and spread over casserole. Bake at 350 degrees for 35 to 40 minutes. Makes 8 to 10 servings.

Topping:　　　　1 cup brown sugar
　　　　　　　　⅓ cup flour
　　　　　　　　½ cup butter
　　　　　　　　½ to 1 cup chopped pecans

FROM THE KITCHEN OF: Shelby Wilhelm
RECIPE FOR: Spiced Beets and Eggs
INGREDIENTS:　　1 cup beet juice
　　　　　　　　1 cup vinegar
　　　　　　　　1 cup sugar (brown and white mixed)
　　　　　　　　Dash of cloves
　　　　　　　　Dash of cinnamon
　　　　　　　　2 cans beets
　　　　　　　　Hard-cooked eggs

Combine all ingredients in saucepan and heat until sugars dissolve.

Remove from heat and cool about one-half hour, then pour over beets. Add hard-boiled eggs to this and let sit several days in refrigerator.

FROM THE KITCHEN OF: Naomi Sterner
RECIPE FOR: Oven Baked Potatoes
INGREDIENTS: 2 eggs beaten
                     ¼ cup flour
                     ½ tsp. baking powder
                     1 tsp. salt
                     ¼ tsp. pepper
                     ½ cup chopped onion
                     8 medium potatoes, pared and shredded
                     ¼ cup melted butter
                     Paprika

Combine first 5 ingredients. Add onion, potatoes and butter. Mix well. Turn mixture into greased 9-inch square baking dish. Sprinkle with paprika. Bake in 350 degree oven one hour or until potatoes are tender and top is brown. Makes 4 to 6 servings.

FROM THE KITCHEN OF: Marian Nash
RECIPE FOR: Swiss Bliss
INGREDIENTS: Strips of chuck steak
                     ½ envelope dry onion soup
                     ½ green pepper
                     Sliced mushrooms
                     1 lb. tomatoes, drained, chopped and reserve liquid
                     1 tbsp. cornstarch
                     1 tsp. Worcestershire sauce

Spray an 8 x 8 inch baking pan with Pam. Lay meat in shingle arrangement in pan. Arrange the dry soup mix, green pepper, mushrooms and tomatoes over the meat. Mix cornstarch and Worcestershire sauce in the reserved liquid. Mix well. Pour over the meat mixture. Cover with Reynolds Wrap and bake at 345 degrees for 2 hours.

FROM THE KITCHEN OF: Bonnie Ferrier
RECIPE FOR: Baked Seafood Casserole
INGREDIENTS: 3 cups cornflakes
                     3 tbsp. melted butter
                     12 to 16 oz. backfin crab meat

2 cups diced, cooked shrimp
½ cup chopped green pepper
¼ cup chopped onion
1 cup chopped celery
1 cup mayonnaise
½ tsp. salt
2 tsp. Worcestershire sauce

Crush cornflakes. Mix with butter and set aside. Combine crab meat and other ingredients. Spread in large casserole (9 x 13-inch). Sprinkle with cornflake topping and paprika. Bake in oven at 350 degrees for 30 minutes. Can make ahead and refrigerate.

FROM THE KITCHEN OF: Marian Thomas
RECIPE FOR: Corn Fritters
INGREDIENTS: 2 cups raw corn
1 well-beaten egg
1½ tsp. sugar
⅓ tsp. salt
⅛ tsp. pepper
1 tbsp. melted butter
¼ cup flour
½ tsp. baking powder

Combine first 6 ingredients. Mix and sift flour and baking powder. Add to first mixture. Drop batter from spoon into a little fat in hot frying pan and brown both sides. Serves 6.

FROM THE KITCHEN OF: Doris Dell
RECIPE FOR: Salmon Loaf
INGREDIENTS: 1 cup flaked salmon
1 cup soft bread crumbs
2 tsp. parsley
1 tbsp. lemon juice
½ tsp. salt
Dash of pepper
2 eggs, separated
¼ to ½ cup milk

Mix all together except egg whites. Beat egg whites and add. Cover with white sauce. Put in greased baking dish; set in pan of water and bake in

350 degree oven for about 50 or 60 minutes.

White Sauce: 2 tbsp. melted margarine
                           2 tbsp. flour
                           1 cup milk
                           ¼ tsp. salt
                           ⅛ tsp. pepper

Add flour to melted margarine and blend. Add milk slowly, stirring. Season with salt and pepper.

FROM THE KITCHEN OF: Geraldine Berwager
RECIPE FOR: Garden Chicken
INGREDIENTS: 1 tbsp. oil
                       1½ lb. chicken parts
                       1 medium potato, sliced
                       1 cup sliced carrots
                       2 envelopes Cup of Soup (cream of chicken flavor)
                       2/3 cup water

Heat oil in skillet; add chicken and brown. Drain. Add vegetables and soup mix blended with water. Simmer covered for 45 minutes. Serves 2.

FROM THE KITCHEN OF: Margaret McCullough
RECIPE FOR: Blueberry Muffins
INGREDIENTS: 2 eggs
                       ½ cup melted butter
                       1 cup sugar
                       1 cup yogurt
                       2 cups flour
                       1 tsp. baking powder
                       ½ tsp. baking soda
                       1 tsp. lemon juice
                       1 cup blueberries

Beat eggs; add melted butter and sugar. Stir in yogurt; add lemon juice and dry ingredients until blended. Add blueberries. Bake at 375 degrees for 25 minutes. Makes 12 to 15 muffins.

FROM THE KITCHEN OF: Margaret Miller
RECIPE FOR: Glaze for Ham

INGREDIENTS: 1 cup packed brown sugar
⅛ tsp. ground cloves
⅛ tsp. cinnamon
½ tsp. dry mustard
2 tbsp. flour
3 tbsp. water or vinegar

Cover ham and bake.

FROM THE KITCHEN OF: Betty Jenkins
RECIPE FOR: Cheesy Beans
INGREDIENTS: 2 cans green beans, undrained
¼ cup dry onion soup mix
3 tbsp. butter
3 tbsp. Parmesan Cheese

Empty beans with liquid into saucepan. Add onion soup mix and cook on medium-low heat for about 20 minutes. Drain and put in serving dish. Toss green beans with butter and cheese. Serves 4 to 6.

FROM THE KITCHEN OF: Evonne Brilhart
RECIPE FOR: Red Cabbage
INGREDIENTS: 3½ lb. red cabbage
2 chopped onions
¼ cup margarine
1 cup raisins
2 large apples, chopped
2 tsp. salt
1 tsp. allspice
¼ tsp. pepper
3 tbsp. sugar
¼ cup vinegar

Brown onions slightly in margarine. Add remainder of ingredients. Add small amount of water. Cover and cook over low heat 2 hours. Makes large amount. May freeze unused portion.

FROM THE KITCHEN OF: June Brown
RECIPE FOR: Crescent Chicken Squares
INGREDIENTS: 3 oz. cream cheese, softened
2 tbsp. melted margarine

2 cups cooked chicken breasts
¼ tsp. salt
⅛ tsp. pepper
2 tbsp. milk
1 tbsp. chopped onion, cooked
1 tbsp. pimento
8 oz can crescent rolls
1 tbsp. melted butter

Blend cream cheese and margarine. Add next 6 ingredients. Separate crescent rolls into 4 rectangles; seal perforations. Spoon ½ cup chicken mixture onto center of each rectangle; pull 4 corners of dough to center of mixture and seal. Brush top with melted butter. Sprinkle with croutons if you like. Bake on cookie sheet at 350 degrees for 20 to 25 minutes. Serves 4.

FROM THE KITCHEN OF: Leda Garrett
RECIPE FOR: Chicken Noodle Casserole
INGREDIENTS: 4 cups water
1 tsp. salt
1 cup noodles
1 can mushroom soup
1 cup milk
3 tbsp. butter
1 cup boned chicken
Bread crumbs

Cook noodles, drain and put back into pan. Mix soup and milk together. Put soup, chicken and noodles together in a buttered casserole. Melt butter and mix in crumbs. Spread over casserole. Bake 15 minutes at 375 degrees. Serves 4 to 5.

FROM THE KITCHEN OF: Alice Sellers
RECIPE FOR: Ham Towers
INGREDIENTS: ¼ cup melted margarine
¼ cup flour
1½ cup milk
½ cup chicken broth
2 oz. American cheese
1 tsp. mustard
1 tsp. Worcestershire sauce

2 tsp. parsley
2 cups or more chopped, cooked ham

Mix melted margarine, flour, milk and chicken broth. Stir and cook until bubbly. Add cheese, mustard, Worcestershire sauce, parsley and ham. Cook until cheese melts.
Optional: Green peas (as many as you like)
Pour over rice, Chinese noodles, pastry shells or toast.

FROM THE KITCHEN OF: Glendora H. Engman
RECIPE FOR: Broccoli Casserole
INGREDIENTS: 16 oz. frozen broccoli cooked and drained
2 eggs beaten
2 tbsp. cornstarch
1 tsp. onion, chopped
1 can cream of mushroom soup
1 cup shredded Cheddar cheese
½ cup mayonnaise
Ritz crackers or ½ cup cracker crumbs

Mix all ingredients except cracker crumbs. Pour into buttered baking dish. Sprinkle crackers on top and dot with butter. Bake at 350 degrees for 30 to 40 minutes.

FROM THE KITCHEN OF: Catherine Myers
RECIPE FOR: Dried Beef Canapés
INGREDIENTS: ½ cup shredded dried beef
1 (3 oz) cream cheese
1 tbsp. horseradish
1 tbsp. minced onion
1 tbsp. salad dressing

Combine ingredients thoroughly and spread on crackers.

FROM THE KITCHEN OF: Jannie Schmidt
RECIPE FOR: Glazed Carrots
INGREDIENTS: 4 cups sliced carrots
4 tbsp. margarine
4 tsp. flour
½ cup orange juice
⅔ cup firmly packed brown sugar

½ tsp. salt
Pinch of cinnamon
½ tsp. vanilla

Cook carrots to desired doneness. In another pan melt butter and stir in flour and other ingredients except vanilla. Heat until thickened. Add vanilla. Pour over drained carrots.

FROM THE KITCHEN OF: Ruth Calp
RECIPE FOR: Melting Moments
INGREDIENTS: 1 cup flour
                ½ cup cornstarch
                ½ cup 10X sugar
                ¾ cup corn oil margarine
                1 tsp. vanilla

Beat margarine until smooth. Combine dry ingredients and add to margarine. Add vanilla. Chill 1 hour. Shape into 1-inch balls. Place on ungreased cookie sheet 1 ½ inches apart. Flatten. Bake in 375 degree oven for 10 to 12 minutes. Makes about 3 dozen.

FROM THE KITCHEN OF: Doris Martin
RECIPE FOR: Never Fail Pie Crust
INGREDIENTS: 3 cups pre-sifted flour
                1½ tsp. salt
                1 cup lard or 1 ¼ cups shortening
                1 egg
                5 tbsp. water
                1 tsp. vinegar

Blend first 3 ingredients with pastry blender. Beat egg and add to vinegar and water. Add to the flour mixture all at once. Allow to stand about 5 minutes to absorb all the liquids. Form a ball with the pastry and refrigerate for awhile before rolling out. This pie crust refrigerates and freezes well to use later. Use a pastry cloth and a cover on the rolling pin.

FROM THE KITCHEN OF: Gladys Lang
RECIPE FOR: Succotash
INGREDIENTS: 6 bacon slices, chopped
                1 medium onion, chopped
                1 medium green pepper, chopped

1 (10 oz.) pkg. frozen lima beans
1 (10 oz.) pkg. frozen whole kernel corn
1 ¼ tsp. salt
2 tbsp. all-purpose flour

About 30 minutes before serving, brown bacon lightly. Spoon off all but 2 tablespoons drippings from skillet; add onion and green pepper. Cook 5 minutes. Add frozen vegetables, 1 cup water and salt and heat to boiling. Reduce heat to low, cover and simmer 5 to 10 minutes until vegetables are tender. In cup, blend flour with 2 tablespoons water; stir into mixture and cook, stirring constantly until mixture is thickened. Makes 6 servings.

Psalm 85:8 "Show us Lord your love; grant us your salvation."

SEASONED WITH RHYMES AND A PINCH OF THYME

IN CELEBRATION OF PASTOR ELLIS KRETSCHMER'S TENTH YEAR WITH IMMANUEL EVANGELICAL LUTHERAN CHURCH

Tonight we take this opportunity
To honor our very special pastor
Who having shared 10 years with us
Has helped us grow in service to our Master.

On July 3, 1968,
The official call was read
To extend a call to Ellis Kretschmer
For by his hands we sought to be led.

One of his first sermons
Was "The Desert of Discipline".
It couldn't have been more appropriate
As an introduction of him.

We have expanded our horizons
And Pastor's discipline has made us grow.
His devotion to his call from God
Has been our reward, as we well know.

Pastor's first congregation report
Was in November of 1968.
He stressed the need for changes
To improve, inspire and impressively create.

So, let's look back and evaluate
The goals he proposed to reach.
Additional liturgy and education
Was bound to impress and teach.

IMMANUEL EVANGELICAL LUTHERAN CHURCH

In 1969, the office was organized
With definite hours set,
A monthly calendar for daily activities
And always the first Wednesday our Church
Council met.

The Society of St. Andrew
Was formed to conveniently provide
Many services performed by acolytes
And sixteen boys replied.

To heighten our feeling of reverence,
And as a symbol of His eternal light,
A beautiful sanctuary lamp was added
Proving to be a very fulfilling sight.

A Youth Service pleased over 300;
Stewardship and Youth Committees were created;
A red rose for all mothers of Immanuel,
And our Mother of the Year was quite elated.

A brand new parsonage was dedicated
And the Brick Campaign reduced our debt.
An open house for Immanuel
Where joy and deep appreciation were met.

Palm Sunday Service was enlightened
With the blessing of the palm.
Kneeling was implemented
With a certain reverent calm.

In 1970 an attempt was made
To expand our evangelism aim.
The Good Shepherd program developed
But efforts were only made in vain.

New Introits and Graduals
Were introduced by the choir,
And the liturgical responses
Were chosen to enhance and inspire.

Pastor went on the air in '70
Over Station WTTR.
"Church on the Air" was the program
And reached many others near and far.

A surprise 25th Wedding Anniversary
Was given to Pastor and Mrs. K.
It will long be remembered by them
As a very special day.

1971 was busy
With new and different means,
Such as the first camp fire service
As the flickering flames were impressively seen.

The new contemporary communion
Was introduced to us.
Along with home-baked bread,
The service was eventually voted a plus.

Palm Sunday brought an experience,
Which was new to everyone.
As we processed around the church,
Our hearts went out to God's Blessed Son.

A new library was completed
And has been an educational arm.
The lovely walnut bookshelves
Give a warm and welcoming charm.

Pastor became part of history
When Immanuel's mortgage was burned.
Dr. Paul Orso attended
And as members, great satisfaction was earned.

Breakfast at Immanuel
Became a first in '72
At Pastor's weekly Lenten Service
For all the youth to pursue.

Speaking of youth and new ideas
The folk masses were introduced.
The youth put much feeling and hard work
In these services which they produced.

With the help of our L.C.W.,
Our lovely parlor came to be.
New décor from top to bottom –
Impressive through its charm and serviceability.

Key '73 loomed large on our horizon
As projects for evangelism were planned.
Our Greeter Program was established
To extend to all a welcoming hand.

The highlight of 1973
Came when our Turk family arrived.
Immanuel excelled with its concern
To keep God's children from being deprived.

Immanuel's stained glass windows
Are part of its loveliest features.
Repairs were made to preserve
These precious stories from the greatest teacher.

Our eyes were opened
And our hearts restored
When Eshelman Studios
Presented God's beauty so often ignored.

New words and meanings came to be
When "Exploration in Faith" organized.
Pastor excelled in his teaching
And group discussion was summarized.

In Nineteen Hundred and Seventy-four
Home communions were given a try.
"Improving the Spiritual Life of our Parish"
Was the theme in which we tried to comply.

The pink room changed its color,
As well as its famous name.
Taking on a fresh look of green,
"The Martin Luther Room" will now be its fame.

A highlight in our Pastor's life
Observed his 30 years since ordination.
Good fellowship and a financial gift
Sent them on a cruise for their vacation.

The Sunday School drew up a budget
For the first time in '75.
Along with many capable minds
Its constitution was reviewed and revived.

Hunger was the topic of concern
Through the World Hunger Appeal.
Pastor chaired the Crop Walks;
Pounds Off For Hunger has been providing meals.

A discovery was made in the bell tower,
Which brought worry and concern.
Pastor climbed the ladder
And evidence of bad news he soon was to learn.

The decay was very evident
So repairs were immediately made.
Many sighs of relief were heard
When all was repaired and all bills paid.

Concern was spelled with a capital "C"
During Harvest Festival this year.
Members came forth to the chancel
Bearing gifts of food and good cheer.

1976 was a memorable year
In which Pastor had participation.
The dedication of our oak tree
Brought grandeur and appreciation.

IMMANUEL EVANGELICAL LUTHERAN CHURCH

A new dishwasher for the kitchen;
A new roof on the church;
Squeaks and lost chords from the organ
Found an Organ Committee beginning a search.

On October 6th of '76
Immanuel's vote was to pursue.
On October 9th of '77
We dedicated a new Moller, thanks to all of you.

This was one of our biggest projects,
As well as a great reward,
Bringing beauty in sight and sound
But not a trace of the famous "Lost Chord".

An outdoor communion and picnic
In Manchester's Christmas Tree Park
Brought many favorable comments,
So records were made of a positive mark.

Pastor has brought many members to Immanuel
If our memories will help us to remember,
But he really outdid himself in this year
With powder post beetles in December.

We had another first in Immanuel
The year of 1978.
The Lenten Devotional Booklets
Were composed by members and rated just great.

A definite vote for contemporary communion,
If revised booklets were provided;
A successful Agape Meal in Lent –
As communion was offered and bread was
divided.

Carroll Lutheran Village was introduced
As a project for our later years.
A big undertaking for one and all
But a way to provide for those we hold dear.

A visit from the Fire Marshall
Saying another exit was needed.
In order to continue with social functions,
Plans were made and work proceeded.

A letter of congratulations
Dr. Orso personally sent
Thanking us for our gift of benevolence
Of one hundred and five per cent.

The ordering of new service hymnals
Is a big decision to be made.
Workshops held and copies reviewed –
Sources provided to come to our aid.

Our first Adult Retreat
Is planned for '79
With lots of fun and fellowship
And plenty of good food when its time to dine.

Now I have only mentioned the highlights
Of Pastor Kretschmer's past ten years.
I haven't mentioned the daily tasks
That are a major part of his devoted career.

The daily visits to the sick;
The many, many meetings;
Chaplain for the day at the hospital;
And WTTR devotional greetings.

Daily correspondence and study,
Bulletins, Visitors and such,
Synod obligations and services
And continual education to keep in touch.

Nursing Home obligations,
Adult and Confirmand instruction,
Ministerial Association duties
Are just small parts of Pastor's production.

SEASONED WITH RHYMES AND A PINCH OF THYME

Now wouldn't you think that with all Pastor does,
And believe me, there is so very much more,
That he just wouldn't have the time
To do ordinary around-the-home chores?

Well, let me tell you a thing or two
That will probably be of no surprise.
He is just as organized at home
As he is in Immanuel's eyes.

Pastor and Mrs. Kretschmer
Have a "window-washing routine".
She stays in and he goes out
And they polish and shine until clean.

Of all the cars on Park Avenue
There are two that literally shine.
The neighbors always know when it's Friday
Because it's Pastor's car washing time.

I bet you think that when it snows
Pastor stays inside and hides.
His neighbors tell us at 2 a.m.
He and his wife are still shoveling side by side.

Everyone needs entertainment
Away from the routines of life
And Allenberry Playhouse
Fills this order for Pastor and his wife.

We all have our favorite entertainment,
And who am I to suggest,
That Pastor really wanted to take
The Foards to see "This is Burlesque"?

You know we often tease the Pastor
About his heavy foot in the car.
Well, finally a good member of Immanuel
Solved his problem – periodically so far.

When the sky is blue and vacant
Pastor takes a ride in a plane.
The wheel is eventually handed to him
But guided by our dear friend, Wayne.

Did you know Pastor is a card shark?
With Canasta if he gives up it's a sin.
Word is, he will play until 2 a.m.
Why? Because he likes to win.

Pastor is also a man of his word
And really this doesn't need to be proved.
When he promises newlyweds to guard their car
Before the car goes, Pastor has to be moved.

Because our Pastor has a sense of humor
I was able to relay
Not only the serious side of him,
But the side we don't see from day to day.

Pastor Kretschmer, tonight we honor you
In this very important year.
Not only for your accomplishments
But your friendship to each of us here.

In your letter from Philadelphia,
Dated July of 1968,
You asked that we march shoulder to shoulder
As we try to make Immanuel great.

The more hands, and feet, and heads together
The stronger and better the results;
Not a pastor's church or a people's congregation
But a team who willingly consults.

Pastor Kretschmer, I think we have done it
Although the road gets rough from time to time.
As Christians we call it growing
And in God's eyes it looks sublime.

We thank you for leading us

And following Martin Luther's example.
As he reformed the church for the better,
Your ten years of guidance has been just a sample.
We pray for your health and your wisdom,

And we look forward to many a year
Of being led by your guiding hands
With our blessings and prayers most sincere.

FROM THE KITCHEN OF: Bonnie Hull in Honor of Pastor Ellis Kretschmer

RECIPE FOR: Roast Duck and Roast Duckling

DIRECTIONS: Rub inside of bird with salt. Stuff loosely with quartered onions, apples. Truss bird if large. Place breast up on rack in shallow pan. Brush with salad oil or lay bacon over breast. If bird is of uncertain age, you may want to pour 1 cup boiling water in pan. Roast at 325 degrees to 350 degrees 15 to 20 minutes per pound or until bird is tender. Baste frequently with pan drippings. Discard stuffing and serve. Allow 1 to 1 ½ pounds per person.

Roast Duckling: 3½ TO 5 pound ready-to-cook duckling
Orange Stuffing (recipe follows)
1 tsp. kitchen bouquet
2 tbsp. honey

Remove wing tips and first joints leaving only meaty second joints. Rub inside with salt. Stuff lightly with stuffing (or you can use celery leaves and quartered apple). Don't prick skin or truss. Skewer opening; lace. Place breast up on rack in shallow pan. Don't add water. Roast uncovered at 325 degrees 1 ½ to 2 hours for medium done, 2 to 2½ hours for well done. (Leg will move easily.) About 30 minutes before end of roasting time, brush with mixture of honey and kitchen bouquet. Roast till done. Serves 3 to 4.

Orange Stuffing: 3 cups dry bread cubes, toasted
½ cup hot water
2 tsp. grated orange peel
⅔ cup diced orange
2 cups diced celery
¼ cup melted butter
1 beaten egg
½ teaspoon salt
Dash pepper
¼ tsp. poultry seasoning

Soften bread cubes in hot water 15 minutes. Add remaining ingredients; combine lightly. Stuff duck. Stuffing for 5-pound duck.

1 Samuel 25:6 "Say to him 'Long life to you! Good health to you and your household And good health to all that is yours.'

132

IMMANUEL EVANGELICAL LUTHERAN CHURCH
THANKS EARL YINGLING

Immanuel celebrates many occasions
Throughout the church calendar year,
But those which have touched us the most
Have honored members whose devotion has been
sincere.

No, our Mother of the Year did not renege
And our Father of the Year we have yet to
celebrate.
But, today a pillar of Immanuel sits among us
Whose support and devotion we truly appreciate.

When deciding how to begin this presentation,
My favorite poem came to mind,
Being a coincidence in work that he loves
And a reality of his strength so defined.

With acknowledgement to Joyce Kilmer
I would like to share this rhyme
To set the appropriate scene for Earl Yingling,
The one whom we honor at this time.

"I think that I shall never see
A poem lovely as a tree,
A tree whose hungry mouth is pressed
Against the earth's sweet flowing breast.

A tree that looks at God all day
And lifts her leafy arms to pray,
A tree that may in summer wear
A nest of robins in her hair

Upon whose bosom snow has lain
Who intimately lives with rain.
Poems are made by fools like me,
But only God can make a tree."

Let's begin when Earl was just a seedling
Needing nurturing and constant attention
To keep from picking on baby sister Deanie
And from tearing apart any mechanical invention.

Sister Pauline wasn't left out
Because he loved to get into her perfume,
But, Mr. Bob Koontz soon laid the rules
When Earl was seated in Wentz's school room.

His mom and dad had a public sale
When he was 3 or 4 years old.
While the sale was taking place,
Earl passed out sale bills of what was being sold.

Now he can definitely tell you
There are times when you must do chores you
really dislike
As he remembers having to clean those stables
When he would have preferred riding his bike.

Speaking of his bicycle,
Earl was always willing to share a ride.
He bicycled to school to give others transportation
Leaving Earl to get home by bus, but taking it all
in stride.

Wedding bells were heard
In 1936, the 18th day of July.
Housekeeping started at Hilltop Park
Where his dad's roadside restaurant refreshed all
those who were hungry and dry.

Soon a move above George Trump's garage
And how little sister loved to stay overnight.
Iva and Earl never refused her company
Even going to Hanover on Saturday night.

On May 24, 1941,
A blessed event came their way.
Marian was their pride and joy
And has been since that very important day.

To supplement his county job,
The Maryland Forestry Service hired him part-
time,
But an offer in 1936
Found him in the Roadside Tree Division working
fulltime.

Today, as we ride around Sheppard-Myers Dam,
The giant beauties were his babies at one time
As he hauled seedling pines in his car trunk
And endured hard work while watching them grow
and climb.

Earl Yingling became an author
Of a book in 1973
Entitled "The Big Tree Champions of Maryland
Which includes Manchester's old oak tree.

Even though he retired in 1975,
The Wye Oak remains to be cared for.
Earl is caretaker for our state tree
Continuing to do a job which has never been a
chore.

SEASONED WITH RHYMES AND A PINCH OF THYME

On March 18, 1951,
Another seed was planted
Only this time at Immanuel Lutheran
Where their transfers had been granted.

However, his devotion to Immanuel
Started even before this date.
Earl has served us well over 30 years,
As well as his community and state.

He taught Sunday School over 30 years
And served as Superintendent, also;
A dependable delegate to church conventions –
Dallas, Detroit, Pittsburgh and Chicago.

He has preached sermons from our pulpit
In absence or as substitute for a pastor,
And the day he heard our emergency on his
monitor,
His pickup flew to church for an expected disaster.

Many terms have been served on Church Council
And the office of Vice President he held.
Working with scouts and supporting the choir
Are just a few areas where he has excelled.

To include room for more fellowship,
Many helped as our basement was renovated.
Earl put in 333 man hours
Hoping to cut down costs which were
contemplated.

Years later when an addition was made
For the education of our Sunday School,
Earl chaired the building committee
And many of God's children have since learned
the Golden Rule.

When the building fund offerings came pouring in,
The 8 a.m. deposits had to be guarded.
Looking both ways Earl and his good friend,
Grant,
Made their deposit under wash tubs and quickly
departed.

The Town of Manchester
Has always been close to his heart.
He served at least 12 years on Town Council
And as member and President of the Fire
Company,
he played an important part.

Because of his devotion to the community
1976 was a very important year.
The Bicentennial celebration
Allowed him to preserve memories for many both
far and near.

The Old German Church Service
And the dedication of the oak tree,
Were organized and planned by Earl
To begin the 200th anniversary of his country.

Our lovely Bicentennial Gardens
He designed, laid out, and grew.
Fifty by fifty in the shape of a star,
And the flowers, of course, in red, white and blue.

Now, this sounds like his life
Has been one good deed after the other,
But besides his busy and serious side,
There is most definitely another.

Picture a vacation in Williamsburg
And a very hot summer night.
A 240 pound man on a small cot
And not one inch to move either left or right.

IMMANUEL EVANGELICAL LUTHERAN CHURCH

We all know Earl appreciates nature
And this extends to the Chesapeake Bay.
But when crabbing he dips like a backhoe
And a crab bit his toe on Kent Island that day.

Earl doesn't like to hang around a car wash
Any longer than he really has to.
About a year ago he zipped through so fast,
He had to circle around and again go through.

Then there was the ball game
When Earl drove the others in a new car.
While Grant went for the tickets,
Earl parked on the other side of the lake to prevent
a scratch or scar.
When his passengers saw the distance
To the stadium was pretty far,
One made the questioning comment,
"Earl, I hope you know where you put my car!"

During a Sunday breakfast,
Grant had to ask Earl for a hand
To climb the tower and turn the bell over –
A joke played by kids, but no reprimand.

Earl has always been on top of things
And in Elkton, West VA, this remained the same.
When the emergency cord was pulled on the
mountain,
Earl was 8 hours overdue, and so was his train.

Now, hair styles come,
And hair styles go,
But Earl has the cream of the crop
That never gets in his eyes as it grows.

Many good times has been had with Earl,
And shared with me by a very good friend
Who expressed his deep thanks and appreciation
And this friendship, as a strong tree, shall never
bend.

I've saved his baby for last,
Of course another pride and joy –
Carroll Lutheran Village
Soon to be a reality for our loved ones to enjoy.

As President and Founding Father,
Earl's efforts have formed a solid foundation
At 200 St. Luke Circle
With commitments of $520,000 in support and
appreciation.

One of God's sturdy trees was born
And March 7, 1917, was the day.
A tree that "looks at God each day"
And lifts his mighty arms to pray.

A man who lives what he believes
And is an example to one and all
Of courage when tragedy strikes
And humility when praised for duty beyond his
call.

Upon whose bosom each day of life has lain
Who intimately lives with God in good health or
pain.
"Poems are made by fools like me"
But only God can create one who gives of himself
as God gives when He creates a tree.

June 8, 1980

136

FROM THE KITCHEN OF: Earl Yingling
RECIPE FOR: Sweet Candied Carrots
INGREDIENTS: 1 (16 oz.) bag frozen baby carrots (whole)
    ¼ stick butter
    1 small can crushed pineapple
    6 tbsp. honey
    ¼ tsp. salt
    1 tbsp. cornstarch

Parboil carrots until half done. Drain. Add remaining ingredients and simmer over low heat until carrots are soft.

FROM THE KITCHEN OF: Earl Yingling
RECIPE FOR: Saucy Short Ribs
INGREDIENTS: 2½ to 3 lb. lean beef short ribs
    ⅛ tsp. pepper
    2 med. potatoes, quartered
    1 med. Onion, sliced
    ½ cup chopped celery
    1 tbsp. horseradish
    2 (8 oz.) cans tomato sauce
    1 tsp. salt
    1 tsp. parsley

Cut beef into serving size pieces; trim fat. Sprinkle with salt and pepper. Place in casserole. Brown meat in 400 degree oven for 1 hour. Remove fat; add remaining ingredients. Cover and bake 1 hour until tender at 375 degrees.

Isaiah 44:23 "Sing, O heavens for the Lord has done it … break forth into singing, O mountains."

IMMANUEL EVANGELICAL LUTHERAN CHURCH

OUR HEROINE – ETHEL MARKLE

The Cradle Roll Mothers' Class
Has chosen to honor today
A heroine of Immanuel
Instead of a Bible Hero of yesterday.

In a way she is from the Bible
Being an example of our Great Teacher.
Immanuel's little children have come unto her
To hear of God's love for every creature.

Our heroine began teaching
At the age of 16 years,
And 54 years later,
She is still preparing as each Sunday nears.

Her first class was 8- year olds –
Mary Rehemeyer was one of the members –
Known as the Primary and Junior Departments
And located in the social room, if you will
remember.

She was then moved to teach
Children who were 11 years old.
Among them was Henry Hoffman
And many of you, so we are told.

Our heroine taught
Until she became a mother.
When her daughter was two years old,

138

She again taught God's word to many others.
She will remember the church parlor
And believe me, so do I.
This was now her Sunday School room
Where many of us saw God's stories come alive.

She took only two leaves of absence
Since continuing in 1941;
Just time enough to raise a family
With the births of her two sons.

"Oh Who Can Make a Flower" –
A song that I'll never forget –
"Praise Him, Praise Him All Ye Little Children"
One you can hear her teaching them today, yet

Along with her devotion in teaching,
She has served our church in other ways.
Aid Society and Altar Guild
Having led to L.C.W., which she enjoys today.

Our adult choir felt a loss
When she decided to retire.
A faithful alto member
Who sang 20 years on Immanuel's Choir.

Have you guessed who our heroine is,
The lady with a smile that sparkles.
She's here today with her little folk –
Our very dedicated Ethel Markle.

We portray her, salute her, and thank her
For all her effort and time she shares
Teaching little ones of yesterday and today
That God our Heavenly Father truly cares.

Since our heroine is with us today,
We wish to express our appreciation
With a gift to show our sincere thanks
For her Christian guidance through each
generation.

October 25, 1981

FROM THE KITCHEN OF: Ethel Markle
RECIPE FOR: Hog Maw
INGREDIENTS: 1 pig stomach (maw)
                 2 lb. sausage meat
                 4 qt. Diced potatoes
                 1 small onion, diced
                 1 tsp. salt

Mix together and put into a cleaned pig stomach. Close with needle and thread. Place in baking pan. Add 1 or 2 quarts of water. Bake at 350 degrees for three hours. Less meat and potatoes could be used and your favorite bread filling added to one end of maw.

FROM THE KITCHEN OF: Ethel Markle
RECIPE FOR: Chicken Corn Soup
INGREDIENTS: 1 cut up stewing chicken
                 3 qt. Water

1 diced onion
1 tbsp. salt
¼ tsp. pepper
8 ears corn cut from cob
2 hard boiled eggs chopped
Parsley
Rivels

Cook chicken until tender. Cool enough to cut into 1 inch pieces. Return chicken to broth. Make rivels by combining: 1½ cups flour, Pinch of salt, 1 beaten egg. Mix with fingers to form crumbs. Add to broth and boil 15 minutes more. Drop in chopped eggs and parsley.

Proverbs 22:6 "Train up a child in the way he should go and when he is old, he will not depart from it."

SEASONED WITH RHYMES AND A PINCH OF THYME

CELEBRATING NINETY YEARS WITH
THEODORE HENRY HARTMANN, OUR SHEPHERD OF YOUTH

With his heart and arms stretched forth
God said, "Let the little children come to me."
With Ted Hartmann's heart and arms stretched
forth,
He said, "Let the youth of Immanuel follow and
we shall see."

Immanuel grows with each generation
Our youth being the essence of spring.
With time, energy and enthusiasm,
They serve both their church, community and
King.
Enthusiasm is that certain something
That makes us all feel great,
And it need not be for the young at heart,
For whatever age, it's never too late.

Youth need enthusiastic parents
To nurture and make life worth living,
As well as teachers and leaders
Who unselfishly devote their time in giving.

As small children in Sunday School,
A first we were to learn,
Was "The Lord is my Shepherd ..."
Guiding us with love and concern.

Immanuel's youth have been guided
For many, many years
By a devoted member with enthusiasm
That never alters or disappears.

IMMANUEL EVANGELICAL LUTHERAN CHURCH

Whether it was a hayride,
Bowling or a youth retreat,
Mr. Hartmann never failed to add the spark
That brought them back next week.

How appropriate Youth Sunday to be in October
Because this leader's birthday is, too.
Since October 23, 1917,
His love for life has touched many as he grew.

He was the middle child of five
And was born in Baltimore at home.
Violetville had that rural feeling
Which he holds on today as memories roam.

He always loved to ice skate,
And does to this very day,
But as a youngster took a good dunking
On thin ice that suddenly gave way.

Blue Dam was a favorite pond,
As well as Yellor Dam, too.
Even after his mishap,
His love for skating he continued to pursue.

Her loves sports, especially football,
But several times his nose got in the way.
When he tired of broken noses,
He decided coaching was safer than to play.

Her also loved baseball
And ice hockey when the water froze,
But because of his tackles and putts,
You will see a slight curve to his nose.

During a game in the cornfield,
Which wasn't the softest place to play,
He ripped his pants, ran home for repairs,
And ran back to finish all in the same day.

He met his wife on a church scavenger hunt
And their dating was unique for a spell,
Because his mother sent his sisters along
Which, of course, didn't go over too well.

In order for Ted to borrow his dad's car,
He had to also include his sisters,
So when he could afford his own used car,
He made sure there was no back seat for sisters or misters.

Helen lived near Loudon Park Cemetery,
Their occupation for several generations or more.
His sisters weren't too happy when left alone
While Ted escorted Helen to the door.

Ted's marriage proposal was very unique
With a screen door between them that day.
He popped the question after lots of small talk
And her reply was, "What did you say?"

The time arrived when they could make plans
As Ted told her one fine day.
"We can get married now," he said,
"I got a raise and $.42 an hour will be my pay."

And, so on October 18, 1940,
He and Helen became man and wife.
Around the time he was drafted into World War II,
Linda, Teddy and Thomas came into their life.

He worked on the farm in his youth,
And after Polytechnic, a tool and die maker he
became.
Since retiring, but reluctant to give up his trade,
He worked for his son since his trade was the
same.

You could call him "Mr. Fix-it",
Since he can build and remodel just about
anything.
His wife threw out an idea;
He'd grab his hammer and start to swing.

SEASONED WITH RHYMES AND A PINCH OF THYME

Do you own a double swing set?
Well, he built his before they were sold.
Their backyard became so popular,
He put an egg-timer in the tree so the traffic could
be controlled.

In his early twenties,
He began teaching Sunday School.
At six Linda begged to go to "Walther League"
Because "Upset the Fruit Basket" was pretty cool.

While in their Woodlawn home,
Their grandchildren started to arrive.
Ken, Steve, Angel and Lisa
Were and are the apple of their eye.

Hampstead became their home in '74
And Al and Aleita very special neighbors.
All remember the Christmas tree cutting tradition
Rewarding many friends and family for their labor.

The tree was selected
Then cut and decorated,
Followed by a scrumptious dinner
And the singing of carols as they celebrated.

Shortly after arriving in Hampstead,
Immanuel became their home church.
Ted jumped right into teaching and council
And for a youth leader, we didn't have far to
search.

Wherever he was leading youth,
He was their example, as well.
Square dancing, car washes, or Christmas
pageants;
So many of his kids have stories to tell.

His daughter remembers his youth filming
The Christmas Story in costume outdoors
When they realized after the presentation,
There were just a few sheep but shepherds galore.

Our Bethlehem Market Place
Has been a favorite then and now,
And organizing and getting it started
Was all worth the challenge somehow.

Using live animals in the market place
Called for organizing a search.
Rona says she'll never forget her leader
Trying to coax Delilah, the sheep, into the church.

Mr. Hartmann worked endless hours on activities,
And Susan says he was her right-hand man
Whether it was choosing musicals for Youth
Sunday
Or chaperoning at a sports event as an excited fan.

Meetings at Paula's when he brought the Oreos
And his love for M&Ms and peanut butter icing;
But he had to share with Rona,
Because it was just too enticing.

Nothing is too much for having fun
So he joined a can-can line one year.
His wife made his red and black taffeta dress
And paint strainers were used you know where.

If I remember correctly,
He danced in our Mother-Daughter can-can line.
Again, Helen came to his rescue
Padding and dressing him up to look oh so divine.

Through working many years with youth leaders,
He has learned some lessons, too.
Like never allowing Susan to video tape
And never teaching Rona how to canoe.

Video taping youth activities
Are memories he will always have at hand,
But Susan's half-hour filming of a log
He's wondering if he should have canned.

IMMANUEL EVANGELICAL LUTHERAN CHURCH

And I remember a Sunday at the Hull pond
Watching him and Rona in the canoe going round
and round.
They didn't have a paddle to guide them
But eventually they made it to solid ground.

Some feel his next car
Should have a large magnet on the top
So when he drives off with papers on the roof
They won't blow off before he remembers to stop.

How about a volleyball game at Cascade Lake
Or on a sandbar in the middle of a river;
Perhaps a good game of spoons at a lock-in,
Or a day raking leaves as the wind made you
shiver.

The only time they can remember
That he missed a special youth affair
Was a progressive dinner he looked forward to
But falling off a ladder caused him not to be there.

Chris remembers so well
Creating the gold crosses at League.
The polished and finished creation
Is today part of her home that intrigues.

Paula worked beside him
For many of Rona's years.
She said Mr. Hartmann allowed kids to be
themselves
And becoming one of them, as well, as one of their
peers.

He laid the foundation for our youth
Leading them in God's driven way.
If you look at their lives and children,
You will see his influence today.

Mr. Hartmann is becoming a cook
While living with Linda in PA.
His George Forman grill comes in handy
But those cake mixes are just OK.

One day when baking a batch of brownies
To compliment his veggie and meat,
He told his family that stirring the mix
Reminded him of mixing concrete.

G.G. Pop, as his first great grandchild calls him,
Can relax and enjoy the years ahead.
What wonderful memories for Aaron and his
family
And we, too, have those memories as we were led.

On October 23rd, Mr. Hartmann will be ninety
years
And what an example for us,
Living and enjoying God's blessings each day
And putting his life in God's trust.

It takes a special person
To want to take the time
To do whatever needs to be
To pave the way for a child's lifetime.

It takes a special person
In a quiet and sincere way
To make giving such a pleasure
Having patience for another day.

It takes a special person
With a twinkle in his eye
To warm the hearts of children
Being one on whom they can rely.

It takes a special person
Whose spirit never ages
And the essence of his soul
To endure youths many stages.

It takes a special person
To share sixty years or more with youth
Watching and guiding his flock,
A shepherd leading to God's truth.

Theodore Henry Hartmann, you are that special
person.
We honor you today in appreciation
For your devotion to youth
And your ninetieth birthday celebration

October 21, 2007

FROM THE KITCHEN OF: Helen Hartmann
RECIPE FOR: Peanut Butter Frosting
INGREDIENTS: 3 cups 10X sugar
6 tbsp. margarine
1 tsp. vanilla
½ cup peanut butter
About ½ cup evaporated milk

Beat first 4 ingredients together; add about half of the milk. Add more milk as needed to make consistency you like.

FROM THE KITCHEN OF: Helen Hartmann
RECIPE FOR: Wineberry Salad
INGREDIENTS: 1 large or 2 small strawberry or cherry Jell-O
1½ cups boiling water
½ c. wine
1 can whole berry cranberry sauce
16 oz. can crushed pineapple
1 to 1½ cups diced apples or peaches (optional)

Prepare Jell-O. Stir until dissolved. Add cranberry sauce; stir until lumps dissolve. Add pineapple with juice. Refrigerate until it begins to thicken. Add extra fruit if you wish, then stir well and pour into mold. Refrigerate.

FROM THE KITCHEN OF: Rona Haddaway and Paula Leonard in Memory of Theodore Henry Hartmann
RECIPE FOR: Oreo Pudding
INGREDIENTS: 1 pkg. Oreo cookies
2 sm. boxes instant vanilla pudding
3 cups milk
4 oz. cream cheese
1½ cups whipped topping

Crush Oreo cookies and spread half in a 13" x 8" dish. Mix rest of ingredients; spread over cookies. Top with remaining crumbs.

Psalm 100:2 " Serve the Lord with gladness, come before His presence with singing."

POUNDS OFF FOR HUNGER RECOGNIZES
DR. WILBUR FOARD

In January of 1975, Pounds Off For Hunger was organized as a program to benefit World Hunger where people took off unwanted pounds by learning to eat and exercise properly and at the same time, contributed to the hungry of the world.

During the fourteen years that Pounds Off For Hunger was in operation, over $16,000.00 was donated to World Hunger by approximately 1,213 members having lost approximately 14,290 pounds.

Dr. Wilbur Foard originally supported our organization through submitting a nutritious eating plan and was always available for medical advice if needed and this was very much appreciated.

During one of our banquets, Dr. Foard was our guest speaker and his introduction was as follows:

Do all of you realize
That Pounds Off For Hunger wouldn't be
If it wasn't for a special doctor
Giving us a program recipe?

Two and one-half years ago
I asked "Do you think it would work?"
He nodded his head in approval
And then our ideas began to perk.

Our purpose was so obvious
As we read the news each day
Of the millions that were starving
And needed food in the worse way.

We took a look in the mirror
And saw extras we didn't need.
We realized we could help in several ways
By each day doing ourselves a nutritious deed.

Dr. Foard furnished us with nutrition
And healthy goals for us to reach.
He loaned us a most important tool
That scale which can silently preach.

And then one day a little blue bird
Jogged to my window sill.
"Hi, my name is Tweety Julia.
I'll teach them to run like Jack and Jill."

So, alas, we had a combination
Of exercise and proper eating
And Dr. Foard offered his help
To benefit us at any meeting.

For quite a while now
We have wanted him to share
A professionals viewpoint
On good health and how to avoid despair.

But, Monday nights are busy ones
For Manchester's Dr. Foard,
So we grabbed him on his night off.
Please forgive us, Mrs. Foard.

And, now having been satisfied
With a delicious nutritious dinner,
Dr. Foard will inform us
Why passing up that pie made each of us a winner.

FROM THE OFFICE OF DR. WILBUR FOARD
RECIPE FOR: Nutritional Program of Pounds Off For Hunger
INGREDIENTS:
Meat – 7 choices daily

One choice equals: 1 ounce beef, pork, lamb, veal, poultry
Or fish broiled or baked. No frying.
(No more than 3 beef meals a week. As much fish as possible.
1 ounce meat loaf, frankfurter or luncheon meat
1 egg (no more than 4 a week)
¼ cup cottage cheese
1 ounce hard cheese
2 tablespoons peanut butter

Fats – 3 choices daily

One choice equals: 1 tsp. butter or margarine
2 tsp. Diet margarine
2 tbsp. Light cream
1 tbsp. heavy cream
1 tbsp. cream cheese
1 slice crisp bacon
1 tsp. mayonnaise
1 tbsp. French dressing
1 tsp. oil

Vegetables:

Hearty – 1 choice daily
One choice equals: ½ cup cooked beets, Brussels sprouts, carrots, okra, onions, peas, pumpkin, rutabagas, turnips or winter squash.

Other Vegetables – Raw – no limit
Cooked – no more than 1 cup daily
Fruit – 3 choices daily

One choice equals: ½ cup orange or grapefruit juice
½ small grapefruit; 1 small apple,
banana, orange or pear; 1 med. peach
or nectarine; 2 med. Apricots or plums;
1 large tangerine; ½ cantaloupe; ⅛ honeydew
Melon; ½ cup applesauce; ½ cup unsweetened
Pineapple, raspberries or blueberries; 1 cup
Unsweetened strawberries or diced watermelon;
12 grapes; 10 large cherries.

Milk – 2 choices daily

One choice equals: 1 cup skim milk; 1 cup buttermilk; ½ cup
Evaporated skim milk; 1 cup low calorie
Pudding made with skim milk; 1 cup of
Alba skim milk or hot chocolate.

Free Choices – Use seasonings and condiments in sensible amounts According to labels on items. All other foods not mentioned are not allowed while trying to shed excess pounds.

Drink 6 to 8 glasses of water daily. Limit coffee and tea to 3 cups daily. Fast from 7 p.m. to 7 a.m. (break/fast) Exercise beginning 10 minutes twice a day and working up to at least 30 minutes or more a day. Eat whole wheat and bran foods when specified.

Find a new interest besides eating. Smile – this is the first day of the rest of your life. Live it and love it. Remember, it's not only your body that you are caring for but someone else's.

FROM THE KITCHEN OF: A healthy and fit child of God
RECIPE FOR: Healthy Weight Loss
INGREDIENTS: 2 cups motivation 1 cup of daily exercise
 1 cup understanding 4 heaping tsp. Thyme and patience
 5 cups willpower Dash of humor
 3 cups perseverance

Measure and blend carefully motivation and understanding. Add, one day at a time, your willpower. Blend with perseverance, thyme and patience. Add a dash of humor and knead thoroughly with daily exercise. Bake slowly and remove with extreme caution. This recipe makes a unique and priceless dish and serves for a lifetime if not wasted.

"God grant me the serenity to accept the things I cannot change; Courage to change those things I can and Wisdom to know the difference."

IMMANUEL EVANGELICAL LUTHERAN CHURCH

HONORS TO JULIA BERWAGER

One of the most important parts of our Pounds Off For Hunger Program was the beginning exercise portion led by Julia Berwager. Julia has been a lifetime member of Manchester and Immanuel Church and an example of living a life of proper nutrition and exercise. While working with us at Pounds Off For Hunger, she was inducted into the Western Maryland College Sports Hall of Fame and we honored her with a plaque, as follows:

Roses are red,
Violets are blue,
Would you believe each of us
Spent $11.00 on you?

Now that's what we call devotion
But how often do you find friends like us
Who love to eat, honor you,
And make such a great big fuss.

Now, about this honor
To Western Maryland College Sports Hall of
Fame,

We are thrilled from our heads to our toes
For our Julia Berwager and to her honored name.

We can give awards, too
So, from Pounds Off For Hunger for all your good
deeds,
A Bachelors of Health, Education and Welfare
Because of your devotion to so many in need.

Please don't let this go to your head
Because we can't do this all of the time.
However, we expect you back on the job
Just as soon as you finish reading this rhyme.

SEASONED WITH RHYMES AND A PINCH OF THYME

FROM THE DESK OF JULIA BERWAGER:
RECIPE FOR: Daily Exercise Program
INGREDIENTS: 10 minutes twice a day

Begin with head and work down:

1 - Head and Neck – Slowly turn head to right, then left 5 times. Slowly look up and then down 5 times. Circle head to side, back, side and front 5 times. Reverse direction 5 times.

2 – Shoulders – Life shoulders up and drop 5 times. Rotate shoulders backward 5 times.

3 – Arms and Hands – Rotate arm in full circle forward 10 times. Rotate arm in full circle backward 10 times. Extend arms forward – squeeze into fist and open 10 times. Turn palms up and repeat 10 times. Shake out 5 times.

4 – Waist – Extend arms to side shoulder high. Twist to right then left 10 times. Same position as above – bend touching right hand to left toe, then left hand to right toe 10 times. Bend right arm overhead, palm up, left arm extended down toward floor. Bend from waist to right for 4 counts. Reverse and repeat to left 10 times. Bend forward from waist and backward 10 times.

5 – Legs – Place left hand against wall to stabilize the body. Kick right leg straight forward, sideward and backward. Repeat same to left 10 times.

6 – Feet – Walk on toes, walk on heels. Lift leg, bend knee, circle foot to right, then left 10 times.

7 – Abdomen – Lie on back. Sit ups 10 times. Leg lifts: right, left, both 10 times.

8 – Upper thigh – Doggie 10 times. Touch and life 10 times. Cross kicks, right, then left 10 times.

9 – Back – Lie on stomach prone. Hip lifts 10 times. Cat stretch 10 times. Pelvis lift 10 times. Back press 10 times. Chest lift 10 times.

10 – For circulation and respiration – Rope jumping; running in place; jumping jacks.

11 – For 6 ½ minutes of "overall" exercising use the "Chicken Fat" record.

Julia was an inspiration to us all. She was a physical education teacher for many years, worked with the patients at Longview Nursing Home, and gave us her all at Pounds Off For Hunger.

Micah 6:8 "What doth the Lord require of thee, but to do justly, and to love mercy, and to walk humbly with thy God."

151

IMMANUEL EVANGELICAL LUTHERAN CHURCH

TO THE WORLD'S GREATEST TENNIS INSTRUCTOR
JULIA BERWAGER

Julia was always ready to offer her expertise in any way that she could and in my earlier years, I decided I would like to learn to play tennis. Now, I am a person with very little, if any, athletic ability and I told Julia I would be a challenge, but she knew she could make me into a tennis player. Here is what happened:

The day was hot and humid
And Bonnie was trying to serve.
Julia patiently gritted her teeth
Trying to control her nerves.

Bonnie's toss sailed high in the air
As both heads turned toward the sky.
While waiting a minute for the ball to return,
A bird lost control in Julia's eye.

"To serve we want to remember
To extend our arm for contact,
Shifting our weight from back to front
And trying to keep our racket flat."

"Now, you try it, Bonnie,"
Julia eagerly suggested,
So, as Bonnie was winding up,
Julia's fears were being digested.

"The net, the net," she pointed
As the ball went straight up in the air.
"The ball goes over the net," she said
As she tightly pulled at her hair.

Bonnie's forehand drive
Drove Julia just about crazy
And after 5 minutes of backhand,
Julia's sight was becoming hazy.

"For a change let's volley," she suggested
One very tiring day.
"Do I set it up or knock it right over?"
Bonnie asked as Julia just walked away.

The hours passed, the days flew by
And soon the leaves were turning.
Shoulders slouched, brow now wrinkled,
And Julia's stomach was churning.

"Since one day we could be playing,
Let's learn how to score".
So Bonnie shopped for a pad and pencil
While Julia got in a few snores.

"I'm ready," Bonnie said
As Julia woke from her nap.
But then Bonnie looked at the time
And suggested they stop for a snack.

Scoring didn't come easy
But Bonnie knew Julia was showing compassion
When every time Bonnie missed
Julia yelled, "Love – you've got to smash'um."

And then one day as the snowflakes fell,
Julia suggested something better.
So they sat in the drifts on the tennis court
Rolling the ball back and forth together.

And, lastly, I give and bequeath
To Julia, the greatest of all teachers,
My book entitled "Tennis Anyone,"
Hoping she will be cheering me on from the bleachers.

Written in Fun and Devotion
For a Very Special Lady

FROM THE KITCHEN OF: Julia Berwager
RECIPE FOR: Bean Salad
INGREDIENTS: 1 can green beans
                 1 can wax beans
                 1 can kidney beans
                 ⅔ cup vinegar
                 ⅓ cup oil
                 ¾ cup sugar
                 1 tsp. salt
                 ½ tsp. dry mustard
                 ½ tsp. pepper

Mix ingredients and pour over beans. Let marinate. Add ½ cup or more chopped celery and 1 large onion in rings before serving.

Lamentations 3:22, 23 "It is of the Lord's mercies that we are not consumed, because His compassions fail not. They are new every morning: great is thy faithfulness."

CHAPTER III
HAPPY ANNIVERSARIES

I was honored to have been asked to write several poems for members of our congregation who were celebrating special anniversaries and weddings. Following are the special moments in the very happy marriages of very special people.

IT'S BEEN TWENTY-FIVE YEARS
FOR ETHEL AND GEORGE HOOPER

Today is such a special time
For two people special to us all.
Their very devoted family
Stand proud and nine feet tall.

Ethel and George – you've made
Through twenty-five years of marriage;
Loving, sharing, forgiving
Including the joys found in the baby carriage.

As we look back twenty-five years,
We vision Westminster's Liberty Street.
George and Ethel roomed at the same home
So it must have been fate that they should meet.

The landlady told Ethel
That she was sure to wed
Because every girl who had shared that room
Soon to the altar was led.

"Oh, no," said Ethel,
"Definitely not me."
But, 6 months after meeting George,
She was known as the "bride-to-be".

December 22, 1950,
Was the date picked for the big day,
But without an invitation,
A snow storm came their way.

The Greenmount church is where they were wed
After stepping through two inches of snow.
Rev. Schtolzhauer married them
Before Ethel had the chance to say "no".

Earl and Ethel Hunt were witnesses
On their wedding day.
They remain very special friends
In a very special way.

Ethel and George were look-alikes
In that they both wore brown.
Ethel looked happy and radiant
With a brown velvet hat as her crown.

The old black Chevy hit the road
North Carolina bound.
Upon their return from their honeymoon,
A reception in Snydersburg was found.

Their first apartment was in Westminster
Until George was transferred away.
Ethel said she would move home with mother,
But mother had this to say:

"When George travels,
Ethel travels, too."
So Linthicum Heights
Became home #2.

After three years, a move to Manchester
And they resided on York Street
In a cozy little trailer
With the patter of little feet.

Yes, a baby girl was born
And Ellen was their joy,
Except for the colic pains
Which stayed around just to annoy.

Grandmother Yingling remembers
So very, very well
When she helped to walk the floor
So Mom could rest for a spell.

Ellen finally took to sleeping,
But she had her preference, too.
Instead of her cozy baby crib,
The comfort of the sofa grew.

Soon a baby boy arrived
On Maple Avenue.
Wayne was welcomed with open arms.
Now with one of each, why continue?

For Wayne, walking came easy,
Especially in his sleep.
All doors felt the same to him
As through the house he would creep.

Ethel found Southern cooking
Was very appealing to George,
But the biscuits and gravy had to go
Because of the temptation to gorge.

Ethel found that as hard as she tried,
She couldn't serve George cheese.
Even hiding it in casseroles
Caused his taste buds to freeze.

Ethel will admit though,
He isn't hard to please.
Even his late and dried-up meals
Taste much better than cheese.

George loves to barbecue steak
And we understand does quite well.
He eliminates milk, cheese and butter from recipes
And insists a gourmet cook couldn't tell.

155

George works on construction
And now owns George V. Hooper, Inc.
His secretary is his wife
And Maurice Yingling is the other link.

The children say Dad never yells
When he's around the house.
But, you should hear him on the job –
Like a lion instead of that gentle spouse.

Susanne, their new daughter-in-law,
Is a pleasure to them all.
She has caused a big change
To occur in her mother-in-law.

The kids say Mom becomes emotional
But for moms this is part of the course.
However, Ethel changed her emotions
And an animal was the source.

There was a day when Ethel felt
Animals had their place.
You never found them in her home,
Not even the slightest trace.

But, one day Ethel met Peppy,
Who is her daughter-in-law's pride and joy.
Ethel fell in love again,
This time with a four-legged boy.

Peppy is a poodle
Whom Ethel babysits.
She rises early to take him potty.
True devotion you've got to admit.

The blizzard of 1966
Brings memories I am sure.
They moved into their new home,
Which was a very pleasant chore.

Charmil Drive is now their home
And also their business address.
A lovely red brick rancher
And Southern hospitality blessed.

Ethel and George's friendliness
Has reached both far and near,
Even as far as Australia
When Julie arrived for one year.

Ethel's day begins
Very early in the morning.
The telephone is the alarm clock
And at 3:45 she hears the warning.

She must inspect her husband
As he walks out the back door
Or he will wear good clothes to work
Not suitable for construction work chores.

She has tried everything,
Even hiding his good clothes,
But, he finds them every time;
Just how she does not know.

Ethel has many talents
And not just with her home.
She's worked for the Board of Education
And Sears, Roebuck sales have also grown.

Snydersburg Church felt the loss
Of a capable secretary,
But Immanuel felt the gain
In 1969, the month of January.

She now holds a big job
Working with the finances of the church,
And a finer financial secretary
We would surely have to search.

SEASONED WITH RHYMES AND A PINCH OF THYME

George has a theory he lives by,
The fact that he is never wrong.
At least that's what I was told
From those who've heard it for so long.

But something happened in Pennsylvania
Not too very long ago
When George admitted he was wrong
And Ethel could barely take the blow.

Ethel says it was the first time
In their married years together
When, because of a wrong turn,
He proved he was normal, as well as clever.

George is a very strong person
And looked up to by his family.
He has been on Church Council
And helped plan his community.

He isn't fond of water or dancing
But bowling is his speed.
Perhaps you would like to discuss politics.
Well, George will always be ready to take the lead.

Ethel is ready to dance any time,
But persuading George is a chore.
So, she settles for a TV game show,
But the phone interruptions she'd like to ignore.

George says Ethel will never say she's sorry,
And a perfect example I'm about to reveal.
Remember the pay check you said he didn't give
you
And when found, she thought it couldn't be real.

The good times still outweigh the bad
As most married couples have found.
Shawn, their great-nephew
Is one of their good times when he's around.

Time for vacations are hard to find
But winter vacations work rather well
Unless the weather interferes
Or someone's health rebels.

Remember your Florida trip
When after you had just arrived,
Ellen didn't feel well
And back home you had to drive?

Their children have meant so much to them
And they are as proud as they can be,
But Ellen and Wayne can see things
That most parents fail to see.

Ellen says they were too protective with her
And too lenient with brother Wayne.
That's so normal with child #1
Experience being worth every golden grain.

Wayne is working for his Dad
And a real asset I'm sure.
Ellen is counseling at Junction
And never finds this a bore.

She's attended Frostburg State
And UMBC, too.
Another interest is social work,
Which she also hopes to pursue.

Ethel and George have future plans
And they go a little like this:
Ethel is heading for Florida
And North Carolina George won't miss.

I'm sure they will agree on a decision,
At least we all hope so.
This beautiful couple couldn't live apart
With the love and devotion they show.

I'd like to tell of a warning
Which Ethel gave to the family.
"Positively no anniversary party!"
So, I hope they aren't in for a calamity.

We hope you continue to reminisce
As you cut your anniversary cake.
The lovely couple at the top
Have returned 25 years later just for your sake.

These past 25 years have created
A beautiful and rewarding life
And each of us here today
Convey best wishes to the perfect husband and wife.

May God Bless you always
In your future dreams and plans,
And may good health and happiness
Be forthcoming through God's hands.

FROM THE KITCHEN OF: Ethel and George Hooper
RECIPE FOR: Potato Salad
INGREDIENTS: 5 lbs. potatoes, cooked until done
Cook until not too thick: 4 eggs
½ cup vinegar
1 cup sugar
Remove from stove and add: 1 tsp. mustard
2 tbsp. Mayonnaise
1 large can milk
Beat well together Mix in potatoes and garnish with hardboiled eggs

FROM THE KITCHEN OF: Ethel and George Hooper
RECIPE FOR: Berry Pie
INGREDIENTS: 1 – 4oz. strawberry-banana Jell-O
¾ cup boiling water
⅓ cup cold water
2½ cups thawed whipped topping
1½ cups sliced strawberries
1 - 6 oz. graham cracker pie crust
1 - 4 oz. banana cream instant pudding
¾ cup milk

Dissolve Jell-O in boiling water. Stir in cold water. Chill until slightly thickened. Mix in 1 cup of whipped topping. Stir in ¾ cup of strawberries. Pour into pie crust. Chill until firm, about 15 minutes.

Whisk pudding mix into milk. Fold in 1 ½ cups of whipped topping. Stir in remaining strawberries. Spread mixture over Jell-O in pie crust. Chill until set, about 2 hours. Garnish with strawberries.

John 3:16 "For God so loved the world that he gave his only begotten son."

HAPPY 40TH WEDDING ANNIVERSARY
DOROTHY AND PAUL HARPER

Today we gather together
For an important celebration
Honoring Paul and Dorothy Harper
And conveying to them a hearty congratulation.

Forty years as Mr. and Mrs.
Has brought much happiness to each.
A story of good times and bad
Preserved as only God could teach.

A lifetime of togetherness
According to God's plan.
A man, a woman, and their family –
New generations to share God's love for man.

Let's go back before 1940
To their interesting courtship days.
Dorothy's first impression of Paul
Was that he sure liked to chase the women in the worse way.

Their meeting came about at a party
And later a blind date to arrange.
Grandmother Graf doesn't know where they dated,
But she says it was rarely "home on the range".

Dorothy can remember,
Since they worked so hard each day,
They would fall asleep on the sofa
And awake to the morning rays.

Paul sometimes left about 2 a.m.
Or just before the break of day.
Dorothy and Paul always worried
About what the neighbors and Mr. Redding might
say.

Time soon came to tie the knot
After being engaged for two years.
On Sunday, June 30, 1940 –
A beautiful day that was sunny and clear.

Early birds they certainly were
Because 8 a.m. was the time.
Rev. Rehmeyer was their minister
And Immanuel's bell seemed anxious to chime.

The bride looked so lovely
And her recent diet caused Paul to blink
Seeing her in a white silk jersey dress
Wearing a corsage of roses in the color of pink.

The groom was just as handsome
In his royal blue serge suit.
Ready to pose at Poist's Studio –
Our couple smiled and looked blissfully cute.

Family and friends were ready to greet them
At their reception at Dorothy's Mom and Dad's.
They presented them with bed, spring and mattress
And with good wishes and congratulations, a good
time was had.

Among other wedding gifts
Were two brooms, which soon came in handy,
Cooking utensils, scarves and linens
As well as a picture of red poppies, which Paul
thought was just dandy.

Their honeymoon was very precious
Since time was of the essence.
They were due back to work on Tuesday
So their was little time to make their presence.

Their first night was spent in West Virginia
With Paul's former school teacher.
Mr. and Mrs. Butcher provided the honeymoon
suite
And later Green Lantern Inn was their next
honeymoon feature.

A hitch hiker accompanied them
On their honeymoon that year.
"Lover's Leap" was their last stop
But the end of their honeymoon was no way near.

Perhaps their trip had come to an end
But their lives together continued to flow from the
heart,
And their apartment at the Davidsons
Helped give their new life a proper start.

Dorothy had a hard act to follow
When it came to cooking good food.
She was great with Pennsylvania Dutch treats
But Paul's appetite was always in a West Virginia
mood.

Even though he thinks she is terrific
In everything she places on the table,
Pot pie, turnips and soup to Paul
Could just as well be a storybook fable.

They spent 4 ½ years together
Before welcoming their pride and joy.
Douglas was born December 29, 1944,
A 12-pound bouncing baby boy.

It didn't take long to discover
That more room was needed for little feet.
May 1, 1945 they moved from Millers
To Hampstead at 1730 North Main Street.

Their family again grew when Douglas married
And found much happiness with Darlene Mills.
Now, with Eric, their precious grandchild,
Paul and Dorothy's life takes on new challenges
and thrills.
They both have a sense of humor
That makes their marriage complete.
He teases her about hanging on the telephone
And she teases of his social club at the Gulf
Station as his daily retreat.

How happy we all feel for you
To have spent 40 years as one,
And happier yet are all of us
For your future which starts with each day's rising
sun.
May today always be special
As well as the blessings each new day will bring,
Looking forward to a rich and happy life
As you look forward to each new spring.

May God Bless you always
In your future dreams and plans,
And may good health and happiness
Be forthcoming through God's Hands.

FROM THE KITCHEN OF: Dorothy and Paul Harper
RECIPE FOR: Good Soft Sugar Cookie Recipe
INGREDIENTS: 3½ cups all-purpose flour
1 cup butter, Crisco or oleo marg.
2 cups white sugar
3 eggs
1 cup buttermilk
½ tsp. salt
1½ tsp. vanilla
2 tsp. baking powder
1 tsp. soda

Sift flour, add baking powder and salt. Cream shortening and sugar good. Add beaten eggs. Beat well, add vanilla. Add soda to buttermilk and stir. Add flour and buttermilk alternately. Bake 425 degrees to 450 degrees for 8 minutes. Drop on cookie sheet by spoons. Sprinkle with sugar from a shaker. Cool on wire rack. Store with paper towels on wax paper between them.

FROM THE KITCHEN OF: Dorothy and Paul Harper
RECIPE FOR: Six Layer Dinner
INGREDIENTS: 2 cups sliced potatoes
1 cup chopped celery
1 cup string beans or carrots
½ lb. ground beef
2 onions sliced
1 cup tomatoes
1 cup green pepper

Layer in a greased casserole in the order given. Bake at 375 degrees for 1½ to 2 hours. This makes a good wintertime meal.

II Corinthians 9::6 "He which soweth bountifully shall reap also."

IMMANUEL EVANGELICAL LUTHERAN CHURCH

FORTY YEARS OF BLISS
BEATRICE AND RALPH HULL

In the beginning,
December 1903,
Addie Hoover and Charles Jesse Hull
Vowed to "always love thee".

January 14, 1906,
Wedding bells rang once more.
Mamie Leppo and Harvey Yingling
Were happier than ever before.

On August 21, 1911,
An eager cry rang out.
Ralph Edgar Hull
Told the world he was now about.

August 26, 1912,
Beatrice Yingling was born,
Never realizing in years to come
She's be helping Ralph plant corn.

It happened in Royers Schoolhouse
But they really didn't know
That sticking tongues out at each other
Would make their friendship grow.

Sweet Sixteen
August 1928.
Probably all dressed up
To go meet his date.

And speaking of his date,
She was ready and waiting,
Even if it meant a ride
On the motorcycle when they were dating.

Those were the good ole days
When friends shared good times.
Notice the latest fashions
And the autos to keep in line.

And then it happened
Forty years ago today,
February 18, 1933,
Was their wedding day.

The '29 Ford Roadster
Was bound for Niagara Falls
To begin a wonderful married life
As Mr. and Mrs. Ralph Edgar Hull.

Here they are at Niagara again
The Baughers and the Hulls.
Two years after their honeymoon
They returned to look at the falls.

Their home was with Dad and Mom Hull
For just about a year.
And then Dad made a gift of a horse
When on the Shue Farm they began their career.

The Leese farm was home for a while,
And then the big day came
When they put the first down payment on Hullside,
Because now that's the farm's name.

1935 was the year
Their address was finalized
And in 1938,
Farm help was realized.

So, September 14, 1938,
Their helper made his début.
Pop wasted no time at all
In finding Donald something to do.

On October 26, 1941,
Richard Lee arrived.
His curls were the closet they came to their girl
But he showed them he would survive.

You've heard the saying "we just made it".
Well, they just did when Steve came to Mom &Pop.
He came into the world in a hurry
And he has yet to stop.

Life was happy and busy,
Everyone caught in a whirl,
Babies, farming and babies
And now expecting that baby girl.

Well, she was born in August
Of 1945.
Her name was Charles Jesse
And now a 4th son had arrived.

"Mother, I think it's time to quit,"
He said to her one day.
And, so they did –
But still busy in many ways.

"Get your magazine
And read all about it."
Ralph made the front page
With his corn-drying outfit.

Inside the magazine
Mom showed what was her duty.
Even with all the work she had,
There was always time for diapers and booties.

Running to practice for choir,
Or Cub Scouts and then Boy Scouts, too.
Taking active parts with their sons
Included being a Den Mother in blue.

Up along the river
You would find them having a ball,
Because all six of them
Ran when nature called.

Oops! There is another member
Of the Ralph Hull family.
If we forgot "Ole Smokey,"
It would be a calamity.

Good times included reunions
Just getting together for fun.
The table was overflowing
With goodies by the ton.

IMMANUEL EVANGELICAL LUTHERAN CHURCH

Boys grow fast
As Mom and Dad knows
And what helped them along
Were the weekly 10 bread loaves.

Fried chicken and mashed potatoes
Have always been a specialty
Because of the 2,000 chickens
That were part of the Hull family.

1951 brought a big addition
Which is Ralph Hull's pride and joy.
The pond was something he always wanted
But never had as a boy.

Graduation days came
And it seemed just like yesterday
That the first school bag was bought
And they waved them on their way.

Uncle Sam has a way of interfering
In a person's daily routine,
So Donald was the first to join
The United States Marines.

"Anchors Away"
Was Dick's choice of songs.
The United States Navy
Was where he wanted to belong.

Steve shared the same feeling
And so to the sea he went.
But, you better believe they both headed home
As this is where weekends were spent.

Jesse followed Don's footsteps
And for the Marine he gave three cheers.
But, Jessie did something Don forgot –
He brought back a souvenir.

Wedding bells began to ring
For Donald and Janice Hill
And two months following in August,
Dick and Bonnie said "we will".

That's right, two weddings in one year.
Now two empty beds for the Hulls,
But the two fellows that were left
Surely made up for it all.

Steve was the electrician
And needed two beds any way
To display his many gadgets
And then room for more the next day.

Jesse needed more room
To paste pictures of pretty girls
And to display posters of trips
From places around the world.

Every year was full of excitement
But one year stands out over all,
The year of 1961
When all that stood of the barn was the stone wall.

On the evening of October 20, 1961,
Friends and relatives came
To celebrate a brand new barn
With warm wishes for the same.

November of 1962,
Steven left the nest
And married Donna Shanebrook
Because he liked her best.

You don't lose sons in marriage,
You gain daughters-in-law instead,
And if you don't watch out,
Grandchildren appear, it is said.

SEASONED WITH RHYMES AND A PINCH OF THYME

Scott Michael Hull was the first grandchild
And adored he was and is.
He was Daddy's little shadow
And now a scout like Daddy is.

Scott wasn't alone for very long
Before his brother came.
Brian thinks the world is just great
And big brother feels the same.

It took twenty-one years
Before they got a girl,
But finally in 1966,
Christine Hull came into the world.

We were speaking of Jesse's souvenir,
Well, she arrived as Mrs. Hull.
Teresa has been a pleasure and joy
Not just to Jesse but all of the Hulls.

One day we noticed Teresa
Knitting and knitting away.
It wasn't long and we found out why –
Marcus was on his way.

When Chrisy saw Marcus that did it;
She said she wanted one of them.
And, so in August of the next year,
Gregory Richard became their second gem.

Now it's BaBa and PopPop
And no greater grandparents could there be.
The grandchildren love the farm
Because love and excitement they see.

Christmas Eve is a special time
Each and every year.
All the Hull family gathers
And even Santa came one year.

There is seldom a dull moment
In the married life they've known,
And now after forty years,
The farm and family have grown.

They have always been active workers
In Immanuel Lutheran Church,
And now their interest of traveling
Has sent them on many a search.

If PopPop took another job
Do you know what it would be?
He would take his 14-foot run-about
And head straight for the sea.

He would first make room for Beatrice,
Then the fishing poles and bait;
Next the crab traps would find a corner.
Now it's he, the sea and his mate.

We, their grateful family
Owe so much to them
For the guidance and love they have given
And the few branches they had to bend.

We are grateful to two other couples
Who made this all come true.
We only wish they were here today
To celebrate with us and with you.

Yes, Beatrice and Ralph and
Mom and Dad and BaBa and PopPop, too,
We your family and friends hope you're as happy
On your 60th as your 40th sees both of you.

February 18, 1973

IMMANUEL EVANGELICAL LUTHERAN CHURCH

HAPPY 50TH ANNIVERSARY
BEATRICE AND RALPH HULL

The day was cold and snowy
After the worst storm since 1922,
But this didn't stop the Hulls from showing
How much your family loves each of you.

Served in a private and "cozy" room,
The dinner at Cozy was delicious.
Turkey, oysters, ham and the trimmings
Were plentiful, succulent and nutritious.

A two-tier 50th Anniversary cake
With a corsage and boutonniere;
An original wedding picture for each son;
And a basket of flowers in church to honor this
special year.

We all felt so very humble
Because we couldn't shower you.
What you have done for us during these years
Outshines any of our contributions while your
married life grew.

We hope our marriages will be blessed
With 50 years of close ties with our kin,
And we look to every day we can share with you
As precious as each day with you has always been.

Thank you from all of us
For a day that holds no regrets,
And we look forward to the 60th
But it's our treat, now don't you dare forget!

FROM THE KITCHEN OF: Beatrice and Ralph Hull
RECIPE FOR: Egg Custard
INGREDIENTS:　　7 eggs
　　　　　　　　2½ cups milk
　　　　　　　　1 pinch salt
　　　　　　　　1 tbsp. vanilla
　　　　　　　　10 tbsp. sugar

Beat eggs, add sugar gradually. Add vanilla, salt and warm milk. Bake 1 hour at 350 degrees or until middle is solid.

The Hulls raised chickens and this recipe was used a lot to use up cracked eggs.

Psalm 34:1 "I will bless the Lord at all times; his praise shall continually be in my mouth."

IN MEMORY OF BEATRICE AND RALPH HULL: From Bonnie R. Hull

RECIPE FOR A HAPPY HOME

INGREDIENTS: 4 cups love
2 cups loyalty
3 cups forgiveness
1 cup friendship
5 spoons hope
2 tsp. Each of tenderness, kindness and understanding
4 quarts of faith
1 barrel of laughs

Take love and loyalty and mix thoroughly with faith. Blend in tenderness, kindness and understanding. Add friendship and hope and sprinkle abundantly with laughter. Bake with sunshine. Serve daily in generous helpings.

Ruth 9:1 "The Lord grant that you may find a home, each of you in the house of her husband…"

BEST WISHES ON YOUR WEDDING DAY
RONA AND MICHAEL HADDAWAY

Today a union of two hearts
From a friendship of many years
Learning to know the person within
Along with days of smiles and tears.

Rona and Michael have come a long way
Since their days at North Carroll High.
Just two students in the same English class
And only glances in passing by.

Michael loved lacrosse;
Rona loved the same;
Especially his good looking legs
Which distracted her from the game.

Each went their own way
And years passed in-between
Until their glances met once again
At a fire hall dance making them a team.

Phone numbers were exchanged;
A dinner date at Greenmount Station.
He resembling the diet coke construction man
Was sure to make Michael the Leonards' relation.

Michael loved her eyes and personality
And her strength with life's ups and downs,
But he was Rona's rock
When she needed his shoulder and solid ground.

SEASONED WITH RHYMES AND A PINCH OF THYME

Their memorable date started at Hanover Mall
With a McDonald's delicious shake,
Then miniature golf at Gettysburg
And their first kiss at Blue Parrot Bistro was no
mistake.

On her first birthday with Michael,
She wished for sparkles and glitter.
While unwrapping box, after box, after box,
Sparkling earrings appeared amongst all the litter.

Manchester Hardware will always be special
Where he told her he loved her more than she
could know,
And Wal-Mart holds second place
When he told her together he wanted their love to
grow.

They share a little from each other
And what a magical blend.
God saw that this was good and special
And he said, "This union I highly recommend."

Michael asked Rona to marry him
On July 14, 1999,
Winfield Carnival was the place
Where they would wine and dine.

More sparkle and glitter soon to emerge
Hidden at Rona's and part of the plan,
She had it no other way
But Michael on his knees to ask for her hand.

Today hearts are strong and vows will be said
And a married life begins.
They will walk down a different path
Of decisions, demands, losses and wins.

But when there is love and their hearts stay light,
The path becomes a song.
With God as their guiding light,
He will be there when things go wrong.

May this day bring precious memories
For many, many years,
And may God's love inspire you to renew your
vows
As each anniversary date appears.

"As wedding bells ring out for you,
This message will express,
Congratulations and a wish
For lifelong happiness!"

FROM THE KITCHEN OF: Rona and Michael Haddaway
RECIPE FOR: Peach Pudding Cake
INGREDIENTS: Combine: ¾ cup flour
1 tsp. baking powder
½ tsp. salt
3¼ oz. pkg. vanilla pudding & pie filling
3 tbsp. butter or margarine
1 egg
½ cup milk
1 large can of peaches (reserve juice)

Combine above ingredients and beat for two minutes at medium speed.
Pour into greased 10-inch pie plate. Drain 1 large can of sliced peaches (or

equal amt. of fresh peaches). Reserve juice. Spoon peaches over batter.

Combine: 8 oz. softened cream cheese
                  ½ cup sugar
                  3 tbsp. reserved juice

Combine ingredients and beat 2 minutes at medium speed. Spoon to within one inch of batter.

Combine: 1 tbsp. sugar
                  ½ tsp. cinnamon
Sprinkle sugar and cinnamon mixture over cheese. Bake at 350 degrees for about 55 minutes.

FROM THE KITCHEN OF : Rona and Michael Haddaway
RECIPE FOR: Baked Ziti
INGREDIENTS: 8 oz. ziti pasta
               1 lb. ground beef
               1 lg. onion chopped (1 ¼ cups)
               2 cloves garlic, chopped
               1 jar (26 oz.) marinara sauce or spaghetti sauce
               1 container (15 oz.) ricotta or cottage cheese
               1½ cups shredded mozzarella-Parmesan cheese
               blend (6 oz.)
               3 tbsp. chopped parsley

Cook ziti pasta.

Brown beef, onion and garlic. When beef is no longer pink, drain and discard fat. Stir in marinara or spaghetti sauce. Reduce heat; simmer 10 minutes. Combine ricotta or cottage cheese, 1 cup cheese and 2 tbsp. parsley. Spread 1 cup beef mixture in 1 ½ qt. baking dish; top with half of pasta. Drop 1 cup ricotta by spoonfuls over cooked pasta. Pour 2 cups beef mixture over pasta. Repeat with remaining ziti, ricotta mixture and beef mixture; sprinkle with remaining cheese. Bake at 375 degrees until bubbly for about 25 minutes. Let stand 5 minutes. Sprinkle with fresh parsley. (This delicious pasta dish was served to me during my first visit with Rona and Michael.)

Hebrews 13:4 "Let marriage be held in honor among all, and let the marriage bed be undefiled;…

CHAPTER IV - SPECIAL TRIBUTES—GOD'S MESSAGE

As the sun rises gracefully
On a gray misty morn,
We witness a speechless feeling
Thanking God that we were born.

And after that sun has risen
And the beautiful day is ours,
We find ourselves a witness again
To the feeling of God's great power.

This speechless feeling gives us strength
As we face the day ahead;
We start with a smile and a bright hello
As down the path we are led.

Only a few steps and we desist
For something has intruded.
Still wearing the smile we venture forth
With our Christian teachings rooted.

Soon enough we pick up our trail
And again we are on our way.
But problems and concern arise
Anytime in our beautiful day.

The sky grows dark and dreary
And with problems mounting high,
We can barely see the road signs
As the rains fall from the sky.

We're not alone on our journey
So we seek for comfort and strength;
Since God understands our problems
The dark clouds disappear at length.

As we come to the end of our journey
And our beautiful day has passed by,
Our eyes area focused toward heaven
As our thoughts wander over the sky.

Just as that feeling was present
When the sunrise brought a new day,
This same feeling is still with us
As the sunset ends our today.

Who can witness a day such as this
And accept the troubles and woe?
A Lutheran Church Woman can do just this
Because through her heart God's message flows.

To the Tune of
"THE CHURCH'S ONE FOUNDATION"
250th Anniversary Hymn

Immanuel's first foundation was Zion's Union
Church
Reformed and Lutherans worshipped as Christian
strength they searched.
God's blue prints called for Immanuel in 1863.
Through prayer and dedication, our goals were met
through Thee.

Our oak tree stands in splendor
Its boughs raised to heaven above.
An 18th century landmark;
Strong roots of beauty and love.
It points the way to music;
Our tower bursts with song;
Proclaiming our allegiance, Immanuel – we belong.

Our strengths are grace and service
From youth to adulthood.
Through faith and prayer we follow
As Christ's disciples would.
Our stained glass windows glisten
While telling of His life.
Our ears have captured stories
And hymns of joy and strife.

This special anniversary, we lift our voice in song,
And stand to praise and thank Thee
Our heritage so strong.
Our future lies before us, living from day to day.
Two Hundred Fifty years,
Preserved in God's own way.

April 1985/2010

CHAPTER V – "IN THE BEGINNING . . . "

. . . It started on a hot summer day on August 18, 1957, my sixteenth birthday, sitting on the glider of my front porch with pen and pad in hand. The following is my first poem for your enjoyment.

SIXTEEN AT LAST

Sixteen years ago today
I came into this world
With big brown eyes
And dark black hair
Which was far from being curled.

My life was just beginning
And my future just ahead,
But this I didn't realize
For I was just a babe in bed.

Today you would have the idea
That I was then real husky,
But I only weighed 7 lbs. and 8 ounces
And, of course, was always quite fussy.

As years went by and I started to grow,
I made a big decision
That the thing I enjoyed best of all
Was making me look like a big fat pigeon.

SEASONED WITH RHYMES AND A PINCH OF THYME

Eat, eat, eat was all I would do
And each time gaining a pound or two,
But this didn't bother me at all
Until I later met a fellow named Hull.

Now another year had passed
And I was oh quite proud
For I had been in a wedding
And had made the people howl.

You see my mommy had told me
To walk straight down the aisle,
But to my delightful and pleasing mind,
Each pew I stopped to cast a smile.

Daddy had been away a while
To my small mind it seemed.
By fighting wars and living away,
It was just like an old bad dream.

My first birthday party was given to me
When I became six years old.
With cake and ice cream, gifts and cards,
I couldn't have been happier with a doll of gold.

School days came again at last
And this time I would go.
To learn to read and write real fast
Was my ambition so.

The first day I did a funny thing
So funny that now I must laugh.
I sat in my school desk backwards
And got caught like a scared young calf.

My elementary school days
Went by so awfully fast.
I hardly knew what hit me
When I landed in high school at last.

New teachers, subject and classes
Were all so new to me.
It gave me a funny feeling
That the change was hard to see.

Eighth grade finally passed away
And I in my freshman year.
Only four more years for me to go
And my future lingered near.

That year something happened
Which was such a change for me.
I met a certain someone
Who was available as I hoped he would be.

He happened to be in the very same class
And luck was as broad as was tall.
You could characterize him with anything but shy
Because his name was Richard Lee Hull.

A year before, a rumor had started
That Manchester and Hampstead would join.
We all dreaded the idea
As if at that time we were going.

Soon the last days of school came around,
Boxes of books being packed,
Already to be sent to North Carroll High
As if they thought education we lacked.

Before you could snap your fingers,
Our summer vacation was gone
And here I stood in a classroom
With another new school year on.

Soon the Hampstead buses
Started slowly filing in
With many people just like me
Who felt they were committing a sin.

But as we smiled and exchanged hellos,
Our feelings quickly changed.
We laughed and talked and carried on;
You would have thought we were all deranged.

After that first day at North Carroll High
I wouldn't have left for the moon.
For the wonderful change that had taken place
Was to bring bigger and better things soon.

After a few months had started to pass,
Excitement came into the air.
The kids would becoming sixteen soon
And the ends stood up in their hair.

Sixteen meant to them at that time
Exactly what it means to me,
Because now that I have reached 16,
I feel it was worth waiting for, you see.

So far my sixteen years
Have been such happy days
And my family is to thank for this
As I do when I solemnly pray.

My future is ahead of me
As are the winter snows,
And the path that lies before me now
Is something which God only knows.

Bonnie Lee Reed
8-18-1957

ABOUT THE AUTHOR

I was born Bonnie Lee Reed on August 18, 1941 in the house where I grew up in the Manchester, Maryland area. I was carried into Immanuel Lutheran Church as a babe-in-arms by my mother. I was baptized, confirmed and married in Immanuel, as were my two children, Christine and Gregory. It has been an exciting adventure being able to put the facts of peoples' lives into stories that flow with promises, love, and compromise and ends the way I like all of my stories that I read to end – "and they lived happily ever after." May each of your lives be filled with the love and promise of God, a sure way to live happily ever after.

THANK YOU!

To all of the families who furnished me with the information necessary to write this poetry. To all of you who furnished me with pictures and recipes to include with the poetry in this publication. To Craig Schenning for his guidance in printing my poetry. To you who have shared with me in enjoying the fascinating lives and events of our members of Immanuel by purchasing this book and donating to The Oak Tree Fund.

"Poetry is the music of the soul and above all of great and feeling souls."
Voltaire

Made in the USA
Charleston, SC
24 October 2010